M000202449

PRAISE FOR UP & AHEAD

"This book reflects the authentic Sunny—the unusual strategist. He has the ability to help us discern issues in complex environments and get us to simple yet effective answers. He also has the special gift of communication—many of his buzzwords and catch-phrases have entered my vocabulary!

I recommend this book to any business leader, manager, or individual looking for a unique way to answer a strategic question. Sunny's four-stepper works in many diverse situations. I am delighted that he has finally written this book."

—*Jane Karuku, Group MD and CEO,*
East African Breweries Ltd

"Sunny Bindra has a unique and very effective approach to his work. Many of us have benefitted from his simple no-nonsense, hard-hitting style. His latest book covers so much of what he has taught us about strategy and execution, and I hope it helps a wider group of leaders gain access to his advice. I am sure it will be a bestseller."

—*Dennis Awori, Chairman, CFAO/Toyota Group in*
Kenya and Executive Director, CFAO SAS (Paris)

"Sunny has taught me many lessons, both as an entrepreneur and intrapreneur, on how to become a better, empathetic, and more effective leader. He is always thoughtful in his approach and clear in his communication. I can say with concrete conviction that this book is full of insights, wisdom, and tangible examples of what is effective strategy—and what is not."

—*Dorothy Ghettuba Pala, Manager,*
Africa Originals, Netflix

UP & AHEAD

UP & AHEAD

Use Strategy to Succeed in Life and Work

SUNNY BINDRA

SUNWORDS LIMITED

Published by Sunwords Limited, Nairobi, Kenya
https://sunwords.com

Edited and designed by Girl Friday Productions
www.girlfridayproductions.com

Design: Paul Barrett
Project management: Alexander Rigby
Image credits: Shutterstock/gualtiero boffi

ISBN (paperback): 978-9914-40-371-8
ISBN (e-book): 978-9914-40-370-1
First edition

CONTENTS

WHY DOES STRATEGY MATTER?

"Fortune favors the prepared mind."
—LOUIS PASTEUR

You do it all the time, don't you?

- » Step back from the daily hubbub of your life to take a moment to reflect.
- » Send your mind racing into the future.
- » Have an unexpected "aha" moment when the dots suddenly link up.

> » Listen to what's *not* being said by the people around you.
> » Get real about what you can actually do, not what you hope to be able to do.
> » Match what the world needs to what you can offer.
> » Devise a plan of action to meet the goals you've set.
> » Make things happen, rather than just talk about them.

Whenever you do any of that, you're being a strategist. Strategy is not just for the brainy professor, or the officer class, or the clever hired gun. Strategy is what we *all* do at key junctures in our lives, without calling it that.

We think about what the future might hold. We anticipate trouble. We prepare ourselves for the unexpected. We put something aside for a rainy day. We invest in our skills and knowledge. We try to stand out from the crowd. We make our projects deliver actual results.

We do strategy, without knowing we're doing it.

The Distressing Question

For much of my life, I have been a strategy guy.

I have worked across continents for consulting outfits, large and small. I have led strategy assignments and advised senior executives on how to formulate and execute strategy. I have taught strategy, at business school as well as in my own programs.

My brain is (was) steeped in the language of business strategy. SWOTs and PESTs. Stars and Dogs. Five-Forces Frameworks and 7S systems. Core Competencies and Distinctive Capabilities. Balanced Scorecards and Strategy Maps. S-Curves and Hockey Sticks. Oceans Red and Blue.

Done it all, taught it all.

And yet.

A couple of decades ago I threw in the towel and left the big consulting firms to set up my own practice. I became my own boss and the only strategic decision maker. I delivered my own brand of advisory services and business content. I consulted, advised, wrote, spoke, and taught. I beat drums and rang bells.

All without a strategy!

This startling revelation surfaced when, a few years into running my own enterprise, a favorite client (a leading CEO) remarked to me over lunch: "You know, Sunny, you have walked your talk. Your own business is very strategically driven. I love the moves you've made to position yourself and develop your reputation. Great strategy."

As I started to reply, I faltered. The gentleman sitting across from me imagined I had taken myself through the same processes I had used to guide his company's strategy for so many years. That I had deployed those tools, techniques, and frameworks for myself, to great effect.

And yet, I had done no such thing.

My CEO friend left, and I walked in the gardens of the hotel we had been dining in, pacing up and down and pondering this question: *Wait just a minute. If that way of doing strategy, the one I have been using for years with a multitude of clients, is so valuable and so effective, how is it that I never even attempted to sit down and formulate a formal strategy for my own business?*

Could it be that I *had* no strategy for myself?

No, I clearly did—and that's what the CEO had spotted. I had anticipated certain key trends in the advisory field and set myself up to ride them. I had prepared myself to be a small independent advisor precisely so that I could be free of bureaucracy and big-firm inertia, and nimble enough to try some new things out. I had expanded my visibility by writing a weekly column in a widely read newspaper. I had branched into speaking, lecturing, and writing. I had begun to experiment with social media. I had invested in some key employees and collaborators.

There *was* strategy at work—it just wasn't written down or formulated.

Was it because I had started the practice as a lone wolf and didn't need to write the damn thing down? Was the strategy just in my head and being developed deep inside there?

Perhaps so—but I never once did any formal analysis, crunched any forecasts, or used any of the popular strategy frameworks.

And later, once there was a sizeable team in play, we never once went on a strategy retreat, brainstormed or blue-skied, defined our positioning, set any themes, or constructed any strategy pillars.

We just . . . *worked*.

And so the heading of this chapter might actually be: Does Strategy Even Matter?

This was quite a distressing question to be knocking around in the head of someone whose early adulthood had been given over to strategy. Answer it I did, however. The thought patterns that radiated from that lunch reshaped everything I thought about strategy. They were the genesis of this book.

Strategy does matter. But it isn't what you think.

I mean that in two ways:

One, strategy isn't what you think it is. Heck, it isn't even what *I* thought it was—and I thought I was an expert.

Two, strategy isn't (just) about *thinking*. It's much more than that.

Strategist You

Strategy is done by those who love peering into the mist. What's hidden there? What's coming? What can't yet be seen? What could I take advantage of before anyone else? What do all these patterns mean? Can I connect the dots today to ride the future tomorrow?

Wait: Is this future-gazing even a good thing?

Aren't we all urged to be in the moment? To be fully present? To go with the flow? What is to be gained by trying to anticipate, plan ahead, grapple with the unknowable?

A great deal, actually.

Think about any highly successful leader or organization you have observed. That person or entity is not just optimizing the present—they are anticipating and shaping the future.

» Apple foresaw that everyone in the world would need to have a connected, mobile computer in their hands—and launched the iPhone.

» Amazon foresaw that shopping could be way more convenient than actually visiting brick-and-mortar stores—and launched what became "earth's biggest selection."

» Safaricom foresaw that the future of money was not in notes and coins—and launched M-PESA.

» Instagram foresaw that the most interesting part of the smartphone was the camera—and launched their quirky new photo-sharing platform.

» Netflix foresaw that streaming video would displace DVD rentals and linear TV—and fast-tracked their evolution into the world's streaming leader.

The rest is history. But please note that there was no such history when these brave folks launched. There was only fiction. They had to have the nerve to believe their foresight—and then the grit to move from vision to execution.

It's the same for individuals.

» David of the Israelites knew he could not take the giant Goliath down on his own terms—he had to play a different game.

» Mahatma Gandhi could not outgun the British colonists—but he could outnumber them and shame them.
» Nelson Mandela could not dethrone his oppressors—but he could use the rest of the world to create the pressure and wait them out.

The strategist looks up and looks ahead. The strategist is not distracted by noise. The strategist wonders about the causes of things. The strategist painstakingly assembles the pieces to see the whole puzzle.

> »   Harriet Tubman did not have the reach to orchestrate a nationwide revolt against slavery—but she could deploy her limited means to great effect and become an icon to guide the final revolution.

And *that's* strategy.

Strategy is about raising our eyes from our short-term preoccupations and our trivial pursuits. Or as I tell many newly anointed CEOs, it's about looking up from the trees to see the whole forest and gazing ahead to see the future of that forest.

If that's strategy, who wouldn't want it? We can all be lost in the present and the mundane. We can all get carried away by the immediate and the superficial. We can all focus on what we are able to see without ever observing the greater whole.

The strategist doesn't do that. The strategist looks up and looks ahead. The strategist is not distracted by noise. The strategist wonders about the causes of things. The strategist painstakingly assembles the pieces to see the whole puzzle.

This book is about making *you* that strategist.

I have written it to help you get better at strategy, easily and naturally, without any unnecessary theory or jargon—even if you have never been taught a single strategy course. And if you have learned strategy formally, it will help you to unlearn all that was unnecessary, so that the necessary can take prominence.

Let's get started.

WHAT'S WRONG WITH STRATEGY?

"There is a lot of dancing, waving of feathers, and beating of drums. No one is exactly sure why we do it, but there is an almost mystical hope that something good will come out of it."
—ERIC D. BEINHOCKER AND SARAH KAPLAN

Strategy really matters, but it's broken. For most people and most organizations, it just doesn't work.

Executives go away on fun-filled jamborees once a year and think they've done strategy. They sit through days of mind-numbing slide decks full of charts and numbers and think they've done strategy. They create financial projections for the next five years and think they've done strategy. They pay top dollar for outside consultants and think they've done strategy. They benchmark against competitors and think they've done strategy. They get sign-off from their boards on what is no more than a business plan and think they've done strategy.

None of that is strategy.

The quotation at the beginning of this chapter comes from two consultants writing in (what was then) the *McKinsey Quarterly* all the way back in 2002. It made me LOL before I knew what LOL meant. If you work for a large organization, you were probably squirming as you read it. This is indeed what strategy was then, and what it mostly remains today: a mind-numbing ritual that adds little value but is done anyway, year after year after year. Because that's the way it's always been done . . .

Please understand: if your strategy is boring, you're doing it wrong!

If you're a senior executive, strategy should be the most interesting, most energizing, most intellectually satisfying thing you do. It should be when you come to life and have the most fun. It should be demanding but also playful. Strategy sessions should be animated, engaging, full of laughter.

If you have reduced your strategy-setting process to slow-motion death by PowerPoint, you really need to rethink it completely.

Before we do that, however, let's take a closer look at what's really wrong with strategy.

It's Too Complicated

Or rather, it's been made too complicated. Business-school professors and strategy consultants carry the blame here. Every couple of years a whole new (ahem) way of looking at strategy captures the zeitgeist. A new article in the *Harvard Business Review* leads to a new book, which leads to new tools and techniques, which lead to . . . what?

Once upon a time, strategy was just SWOT analysis, which was so easy to do that anyone could do it. And everyone did. To no effect. Then came something a little more complicated: Michael Porter's Five Forces model, which helped you understand the power structures of your industry. After that you needed to figure out what your Core Competencies were, the bedrock of your success. That was not enough, though: you also needed to create a Strategy Map and a Balanced Scorecard. But wait, Blue-Ocean Strategy was also in vogue, forcing you to rethink where you were competing and why. And don't forget a snazzy vision statement, distinct from your jaunty mission statement, to complete the look.

Don't get me wrong. I have great respect for academic research and the rigorous setting and testing of theory. But all those research papers and articles and books are for us strategy wonks. What do they mean to you, just a good ol' guy or gal trying to be strategic and craft a strategy that actually guides your organization or life?

All of that complex razzmatazz usually means this: that you have to get the profs or the consultants in to help you do strategy in the suddenly fashionable way everyone else is doing it. Your chances of being able to do this yourself, in the manner spelled out in the trendy new approach, are close to . . . zero. You'll need help. And you'll pay for it.

The big bad secret? In essence, strategy is simple.

Maybe that's why.
The big bad secret? In essence, strategy is simple.
(But it's not easy. More on that later.)

It's Secretive

Who gets into the strategy room? It's a hallowed, exclusive club. A popular way to think about strategy is that it is "the art of the general." It's big-picture stuff, done by the folks who make the big decisions. And you can't have too many generals.

This depiction has, unfortunately, persisted. To get an invite to the company's annual strategy retreat means you've arrived. You now get to be one of the big dogs relieving themselves in the tall grass, if I may misappropriate a line from a famous movie. You get to shape the future. Most people don't. Oh, and shhh: whatever you discuss is a closely guarded secret.

The problem? Strategy is done by humans, through other humans. The "generals only" stuff was fine in the military back in the day, when everyone else was handled on a "need to know" basis and orders issued had to be obeyed without question.

Maybe I'm wrong, but I'm not seeing that working out too well in organizations that aren't actually at war, and that are soon to be overrun by Gen Z types who have grown up dissenting to everything, where the ability to think creatively, collectively, may become the only enduring advantage.

It's Seasonal

Early in my career as a strategy guy, I observed the weird seasonality of the process. People would pick a time of year, usually in Q4, to take a select team to a mountain, an ocean, or a lake. A facilitator was hired to take the senior honchos through some kind of intellectually rigorous (though this was often optional) process of brainstorming, filtering, evaluating, and wordsmith-ing.

Finally, on the afternoon of the final day, just before the gala party night, all those gathered would gaze upon it with satisfaction: the five-year strategy.

To be reviewed every year—same month, different mountain.

And then to be rebooted in year four.

I was often that facilitator. It was fun to take all those teams to all those exotic locations, but it was hardly fulfilling. Why? Because the rest of the year had nothing to do with strategy. The rest of the year was for budgeting, running operations, and reporting. You're asking about strategy, dude? It's June. Busy-busy with H1 reporting. Let's talk strategy in November. Shall we do ocean this time?

Strategy is not a fruit that comes in season once a year. It happens every day. It is either in the mainstream and bloodstream of the organization, or it doesn't exist—except as a misnamed enjoyable annual excursion.

Sure, there's a case to be made for taking time to reflect together and bond. Deep thinking and kinship are indeed essential components of a collective strategy. *But* don't ever think the retreat is where the strategy is made. Important work can be done there, certainly. You do some of the essential thinking away from the bustle of your daily schedules. You isolate the top challenges. You craft a working model of your strategy. You prioritize some time and spend. (There's more on strategy retreats in chapter 9.)

What you do during the retreat is prepare your mind for the place where the strategy will *actually* be completed: back at work, in corridors and around watercoolers; in Zoom team meetings and on work chat forums; in candid conversations with customers; in watching a fast-changing market; in getting budgets approved.

To do strategy properly, you have to do it all the time, in all sorts of ways, everywhere—not just once a year in a special place.

It's Outsourced

The single worst way to do strategy is to hand it to outsiders.

Given the continuing size and success of huge strategy-consulting practices, one surmises that it is done this way by many.

Like I wrote earlier, I have been one of those consultants. I have run large projects with swarms of analysts, to craft the strategy on behalf of Megacorp this or that. We were rigorous. We ran joint teams populated by consultants and client staff. We created steering committees. We crunched numbers. We ran scenarios. We prepared snappy slide decks, with many charts and polished language. We presented to the board, got approvals, and left with the applause ringing in our years. Check received; job done.

Not.

What happens next, when the strategy consultants go home? The in-house power-holders take over. They make decisions based on their own instincts; they set budgets according to their emerging realities. Quarterly board meetings are time bound, and they often focus on backward-looking nitty-gritty stuff, like audits, compliance problems, staff turnover—not strategy.

What about behavior? Do people behave in accordance with the new strategy, true to its new demands? Nope. They behave according to their *culture*. As I'm fond of tweeting, strategy is what you think you'll do; culture is what you'll actually do. Culture is deeply embedded in most organizations; strategy is often just froth on the surface.

The problem with making strategy this occasional, expensive exercise is that it doesn't actually achieve anything. The people who work at your organization didn't come up with the strategy, so they don't connect with it. It's not in any language that an ordinary human can understand, so they feel nothing for it. The strategy is a deck shown to the board and investors. What most employees respond to, as they always have, is a different list: signals from their bosses; targets and incentives; the prevailing emotional climate.

Strategy works only when it involves everyone and when it ripples through everything. Once a strategy is set, it must percolate into leadership behaviors, into personal goals and performance indicators, and into everyday decisions. It must be visible every day, in how people work and meet and interact.

No outsider can do that for you.

Is there any role for outsiders in strategy, then? Yes indeed. More later—in chapter 9, specifically.

It's All Brains, No Heart or Soul

If you think strategy is mostly about brains, you will assemble brainy people to create it. If those clever folks know very little about the rest of the strategy equation, they will fail. They might do lots of great analysis for you; they might logically isolate all the options available to you; and they might evaluate your capacities to deliver the strategy very competently.

Strategy works only when it involves everyone and when it ripples through everything.

And still nothing much might happen. Indeed, that's probably the most likely outcome.

Strategy is not (just) something you do in your head; it's something you do with other human beings. Those other humans have to understand the logic, feel the emotion, *and* become compelled to do it.

In other words, and as Aristotle pointed out millennia ago: if you want to persuade anyone to see your point of view or do your bidding, use *logos*, *pathos*, and *ethos*.

Logos appeals to the head—it makes rock-solid sense.

Pathos appeals to the heart—it stirs feelings.

Ethos deploys the authority of the persuader—it bestows credibility on what is being asked of others.

Most of the strategies I have seen constructed by large organizations, over a long career of staring at them, are just logos, period. They have many fancy charts and diagrams. They have lots of numerical targets and performance metrics. They show intricate time paths to success.

Pathos? This is a workplace. We don't do feelings here.

Ethos? This is your boss talking, so you will do this.

And so they fall flat. The people who are asked to execute strategy didn't come up with the ploys or the numbers—they don't care about them. They feel nothing for the glossy document or the flashy presentation. They settle back into familiar working patterns and comfortable modes of behavior—even if the strategy envisaged a radical shift in the approach to the market.

A year later an angry board notices no real change in the business, despite the bold intentions it signed off to. The chairman gives the CEO an uncomfortable dressing down. An angry CEO comes out of the board meeting, assembles senior heads, and knocks them together, warning that some may roll.

The strategy is revisited, perhaps with a different consultant doing the advising. Some of the bolder propositions are now deemed unrealistic. Some tweaking and fiddling is done. A watered-down version is presented, perhaps framed with sentences like "feet firmly on the ground." A fresh rollout is announced, with some of the more ambitious thrusts taken out. The business continues pretty much as usual, making some incremental, timid changes—while living under the delusion that it actually has a strategy.

———————————

There's a lot wrong with strategy. Let's start to fix it.

THE RIGHT WAY TO DO STRATEGY

"The role of a plan is to give you the nerve to race onto the field."
—TOM PETERS

Strategy is the light you shine into the darkness ahead of you. It helps you see what lies in wait—the pathways as well as the hazards. It's your journey guide.

Having a strategy before you set off means you have studied the terrain; you have assessed your own capacity for the journey; you have noted who has gone before you and what might have happened to them; you have created a rough map of the paths you hope to take; and you have the all-important flashlight.

Thus armed, you set off, learning as you go.

Any strategy must be imperfect— as a design feature.

A fundamental point: there is no perfect strategy available to you, just waiting for you to find it. As I pointed out in the last chapter, strategy involves the intellect, certainly; but the biggest mistake many make is to regard it as an intellectual exercise, period.

Strategy isn't what you *think*.

Any strategy must be imperfect—*as a design feature*. Don't even attempt perfection; create a loose script. Your strategy may even be badly flawed—but if you can't see the flaw at the point of launching it, you must press on regardless.

Strategy is an act of learning.

Henry Mintzberg was one of strategy's earliest (and most entertaining) contrarians. Reading the 2005 book he edited, *Strategy Bites Back*, I clapped when he warned that strategies can be to organizations what blinders are to horses. The idea is not to keep going in a straight line while cutting out all peripheral vision!

Strategy is not a straitjacket that you put on and don't take off for five years.

It is best understood as a (hopefully) *consistent pattern of ideas and action*. It is a position taken based on a set of beliefs. Knowing those positions and beliefs requires contemplation—but also the willingness to be wrong.

Strategies are lived, not planned. They are fictions, not facts. Contact with reality—in the form of employees, customers, and competitors—will reveal the lessons that must be learned.

Strategies are tested on the ground, not in the boardroom.

Look at the excellent Tom Peters quotation (it was actually a tweet) that introduced this chapter. You're not supposed to have your strategy perfected *before* playing the game; all you have to do is craft enough of a game plan to give you the confidence to run out onto the pitch.

Once the game begins, any number of things might happen:

> » You might find a hostile crowd that hates your style of play.
> » You might find a biased referee blowing the whistle against you every time.
> » You might find the playing field is tilted against you.
> » You might find an opponent who's got a superior formation.
> » Or you might find you did just fine!

Whatever you find, you weren't going to find it in the dressing room. You only discover it out on the field. Therefore, strategy isn't just what you *think*—it's also what you *learn* as you *do*.

In their illuminating book *Radical Uncertainty*, two outstanding professors of economics, John Kay and Mervyn King, point out that real people (households, businesses, governments) don't "optimize"—they just cope! They make incremental decisions based on lessons they have learned. They try to get better as they go. They don't always aim for the highest peaks or even know where those peaks are. They just try to seek a higher place than they occupy now.

Here Comes the Four-Stepper

So how on earth do you do it, this seemingly amorphous, ethereal thing called strategy? How do you muster enough nerve to get onto the field of play?

We must give it some shape and substance if we are to work with it.

Let's start with a definition: the shortest possible one. Another interesting professor, Bill Barnett, came up with this:

> **Strategy is the logic that
> drives action.**

And that's it!

Please note that you need to begin with some strong logic. Strategy is not witless. It requires both deep observation and careful reflection. Even though strategy is learn as you go, it helps to start from a position of clarity and sound judgment. Good strategies are not built on hopes and prayers.

But we've always known that. The second half of the definition is where it gets interesting. *Drives action.* Strategy is not some sterile thought experiment; it must lead to actual results on the ground. Its impact must be felt by human beings; lives must change because of the strategy. Actions must ensue, and they must provide the data from which to learn and adjust.

Note also that *driving* has a particular meaning here. It might have meant *commanding* in the battlefields of yore, but good luck with ordering young people today to simply do as they are told, no questions asked. In the era in which you, today's reader, will be driving action, you will need to do it through willing and enthusiastic engagement.

If you accept *logic + action* as our working definition, let's get into the heart of the matter and the core of this book: the strategy four-stepper.

Strategy is the answer to four essential questions:

1. What's *really* going on here?
2. Where do we play this game, and how do we win it?
3. How do we make the key people care about this strategy and make it their own?
4. How do we get this show on the road?

Look at the sequence. First, you try to figure out what's going on in the world around you—the opportunity and also the challenge. Next, you match that to your own capabilities and take a position. Then, you try to inspire action in others, because you won't do this alone. And finally, you actually try to do something.

And that's it! Your answers to the four questions are your strategy.

I hope you can see that this approach to strategy is entirely intuitive. It accords with how we, as individu-

---

Study the world and its unmet needs carefully; understand yourself and your own distinctive strengths deeply; and combine the two uniquely. Strategy done.

---

als, address the key challenges of our lives. We spend a bit of time figuring the situation out; we work out what we are able to do; we create a narrative that makes sense of the situation; and then we get going.

In other words: study the world and its unmet needs carefully; understand yourself and your own distinctive strengths deeply; and combine the two uniquely.

Strategy done.

Now you have given yourself a fighting chance of making it.

The table below summarizes the four-stepper:

THE STRATEGY 4-STEPPER	
1. DIAGNOSIS	What's *really* going on in our world, and what we need to *become*.
2. POSITIONING	*Where* we choose to play, and *how* we think we might win, based on our unique resources.
3. STORY	How we will *explain* this to our people and *excite* them with it.
4. ACTIONS	The *concerted* action sets we need to make this strategy *happen*.

Strategy is those four things, in lockstep: a diagnosis; a positioning; a narrative; and a set of actions.

This, I hasten to add, is not new. In my view, strategy has always been about humans trying to make sense of the challenges that face them, and then using their strengths (and overcoming their weaknesses) to meet those challenges. Strategic thinkers throughout history have known this to be the essence of strategy. All I am doing in this book is clarifying and demystifying that which is already known and giving readers a simple way to draw up their own strategies. I am not adding a whole new strategy framework to what is already a long list; I am only distilling the essence of strategy, in four simple steps.

An important caveat: the four steps are not a magical path to great strategy. Doing business, and working in organizations, is messy and unpredictable. There are no natural laws to follow. There are no blueprints to use. There are no formulae that create the desired result. If those things existed, everyone would follow them, and everyone would succeed.

The four steps merely give you a structured way of thinking and acting strategically. They give you a shot at strategic success. Success will swing on how you take your shot—and on a big dose of luck.

The next four chapters will now explain each of the components of strategy in turn.

Let's go.

FIRST STEP: FRAME THE CHALLENGE

"Many of the most inspiring people start in a place of uncertainty, are filled with doubt, yet arrive triumphant at places in life they could not see when they set out."
—MARGARET HEFFERNAN

Strategy begins with a *diagnosis* that confirms what we are up against. Professor Richard Rumelt, in his excellent book *Good Strategy/Bad Strategy*, recommended that all strategic discussions should commence with a diagnosis to explain the challenge being faced in order to understand which parts of a complex reality are actually critical.

Managers are very good at making very long lists of the forces in the environment that must be addressed. Take a group of them to the aforementioned lake or mountain, and they will fill entire flip charts with important factors affecting their future—changes in consumer trends, shifting economic realities, bewildering technological advances, new competitor activity, unpredictable political change.

That long list is futile. Life is complicated, and it has always been thus. None of us can look into the future with any certainty. The best we can do is make our best guesses about what might be coming—and accept that they are always just guesses.

Those guesses are at the heart of being a good strategist.

We make guesses about the future all the time. Getting married, having children, changing jobs, buying that house—these are decisions based on a particular diagnosis: it's time to settle down; I can have a better career elsewhere; I need more space for what's coming in my life. Thinking about the future is not alien to us—we do it instinctively.

And yet, "ineradicable uncertainty remains inherent to human life," says Margaret Heffernan in *Uncharted*, another book that should be read by all strategists. Our need for certainty in our futures—to be able to plan and anticipate and manage our lives—causes us to believe in prediction. We have always looked for those who can soothe us with their predictions: priests, prophets, shamans, oracles, and astrologers have done a roaring trade for centuries!

This belies the unpredictability that is the essence of human existence. For any number of reasons, most of what we predict is simply wrong.

How Wrong I Was

I will never forget that day.

The sun was rising on November 9, 2016, and I was at Nairobi's international airport, heading to Cape Town. It was the morning after the US presidential election, and the early results were coming in. I glanced at the TV monitors in the departure lounge and got a surprise. Hillary Clinton, the clear favorite for most of the race, seemed to be faltering, and the maverick Republican candidate, Donald Trump, was putting in a strong showing.

This cannot be happening, I thought to myself. I had barely paid attention to the campaign, unable to stomach the antics of a man I couldn't stand. Yet there he was, showing up very strongly at the ballot . . . *surely not*, I thought.

It was time to board the plane, and I could follow the election updates no more. I switched off my devices and settled down to read a book, as I usually do on airplanes. The Kenya Airways flight made a brief stop at Livingstone, in Zambia, and a few passengers got off. As they stood in the aisle waiting for the aircraft door to be opened, they connected to the local mobile signal. One of them gaped at his phone and shouted a four-letter word at the top of his voice. No more explanation was needed. We all understood. Trump was president.

For the rest of that journey, I put my book aside and just stared out of the window, deep in troubled thought. I had not, even for a moment, imagined this could happen. I had never contemplated that America, after the historic achievement of making an African American their president for two terms, would flip and give the office to this man of all people, someone who throughout his campaign had made no apologies for his racism and misogyny.

How wrong I had been.

I was on my way to facilitate a strategy event for a pan-African organization, and yet I had been caught napping on one of the biggest events of the epoch. Very humbling. I spent the next two hours telling myself I would figure this out. This thing must have been hidden in plain sight, yet I had missed it. Why?

Over the next few months, I learned a great deal. I listened to the voices I had been ignoring; I read deeper analyses of the state of America; I began to understand more.

I learned about the intense anger in many parts of the US heartland about globalization and its consequences on local jobs.

I began to see how social media was creating cocoons and echo chambers and how data-profiling algorithms could be used to increase polarization and dissent and swing elections.

I realized how the presidency of Barack Obama, far from heralding a post-racial society, had only deepened the ethnic resentments of a large chunk of the voting population.

Yet all these factors were only part of the explanation. It took a different strategist, not only to call the Trump victory, but to explain it.

Roger Martin is a renowned strategy thinker. In March of 2016, he made a ten-thousand-dollar bet with a fellow professor that Trump would win. On January 12, 2017, he explained his thinking in the *Harvard Business Review*. His main point was this: "A bland Democratic strategy interacted with a clever Trump strategy to put Trump in a position where, under just the right circumstances, he could squeak out a narrow victory."

Professor Martin warned against post hoc rationalizations. We can blame the result on Clinton's fumbles or Russian interference, but that makes us forget an important point: that a Trump triumph was one of the longest shots in US presidential history. The only way to win was to run as a rank outsider and invent an entirely new "product category" in the minds of voters: the politically incorrect candidate. And boy, did he go deep on his incorrectness. He reviled immigrants; mocked prisoners of war; made fun of disability; survived the release of a tape where he demeaned women as sex objects. Had a traditional candidate done *any* of those things, that candidate would have been derailed. For Trump, every controversial utterance reconfirmed his category: I'm not a politician, I don't watch what I say, I don't apologize—and aren't you fed up with these other mealy-mouthed politicos, America? Don't you want to try something new and bold?

His opponents woefully underestimated the power of this positioning. They continued to deplore and decry not only the candidate but his support base—and that only served to reinforce the convictions of that base. Trump made his fresh category big enough to win—just barely.

I came away from this whole experience educated—mostly about myself and the things that can prevent me from being dispassionate in my diagnosis of situations. It was my own biases that had blinded me. Everyone I knew disliked Trump intensely; but the people I knew were not the ones lining up to vote. I should have paid far, far more attention to people who were *not* like me. That's a lifelong lesson for all strategists.

The Traps That We Fall Into

To come up with a working diagnosis of the situation you're facing, you have to get better at understanding what's really going on. Most people, however, are really bad at working out the reality of complex situations. We're pretty good at the simple stuff, but when it comes to VUCA (volatile, uncertain, complex, and ambiguous) situations, most of us fail to read the signs properly. A lot of that is down to one thing: our own cognitive predispositions and limitations.

Philip Tetlock conducted a long-term study of predictions made by experts. He found that most well-regarded pundits have a terrible track record—no better, in his memorable phrase, than chimpanzees throwing darts. (This is recounted in his excellent book *Superforecasting*, coauthored with Dan Gardner.)

Tetlock estimates that the US intelligence community spends more than $50 billion every year and employs more than one hundred thousand people. Twenty thousand of those are actually intelligence analysts—they collect data and information and sift through it to see what's important for US security.

That's a lot of diagnosis done by a lot of brains. And yet.

This elaborate apparatus failed to predict or prevent the appalling 9/11 terrorist attacks in 2001, and it failed to find their orchestrator, Osama bin Laden, for another decade, even though he became the world's most wanted man.

This is the very "intelligence" that concluded in October 2002 that Saddam Hussein held weapons of mass destruction, weapons that justified an invasion of Iraq. No such weapons were ever found—but a catastrophic war ensued, and a momentous chain of events was set in motion.

After a lifetime spent with teams of highly educated executives trying to make sense of complex environments, I conclude that none of us can do this thing immaculately—but we can get better at it. We would do this mainly by avoiding some very common traps.

Trap One: Stuck in your own ideology.

We all have big ideas that grab us. There are philosophies of life or work that we find most appealing. We nurture beliefs that we hold dear. These convictions give a frame to our lives; they help us make sense of the chaos; they give us a community of fellow believers to belong to. And then the frame becomes a prison. When we make sense of the world only through our preset ideologies, we see the world only through one pair of spectacles. There is much in the spectrum that is simply invisible to us. Life becomes an ongoing ritual of confirmation bias—we look only for the evidence that supports our own beliefs, and we ignore the rest.

Trap Two: Stuck with your own kind.

Who are your homies, your buddies, your kindred spirits? For most of us, the people we hang out with are very similar to us. We feel comfortable with those who look like us, who believe what we believe, who respond to situations similarly. We choose our friends and partners mostly on similarity, not difference, because we want life to be comfortable and predictable. We tend to do the same in professional contexts: bosses select underlings they can relate to; companies hire people to fit into preset molds. As with our faith system, our regular circle also becomes an echo chamber in which we constantly hear the same beliefs being reinforced.

Trap Three: Stuck in school.

Our education system sets up another trap for us to fall into. Because our education is often expensive and grueling, we treat it as a one-off event to be completed early in life and then concluded. I have met way too many middle-aged folks who are still making sure everyone knows which prestigious college they went to and what they learned there—no matter how outmoded or irrelevant. This ensures that they are stuck in the models and teachings of the past while facing a rapidly changing future—thus confirming their inability to deal with new challenges.

Trap Four: Stuck in the building.
"No facts exist in the building, only opinions" is one of my favorite quotations (from Steve Blank). If you sit on the upper floors and receive filtered information from people outside, rest assured you will be largely ignorant of the facts on the ground. This is a trap so many leaders fall into, without even knowing it. They think of their roomy offices as a perk, and their inaccessibility as a mark of status. But the truth is downstairs and outside, boss—no matter how many cushy sofas and obedient serfs you have been allocated.

Trap Five: Stuck in smugness.
Few things prevent advancement more than self-satisfaction does. Those who are rather pleased with themselves lose all desire to get better. Those who feel the warm glow of accomplishment tend to lose the hunger to do more. It's better to be on edge and dissatisfied with oneself—that's where the spur to be better will come from.

I repeat: these traps are not just for the less enlightened; we all fall into them, often face-first. I know I did in dismissing Donald Trump's chances in 2016. I also know I will be trapped again. The real lesson here is to know the traps exist—that we are often blinded by ideologues, kinship, dead professors, and our own advancement—and to do our best to learn from our stumbles and evade as many of these traps as we can in the future.

Good strategists are never complacent, no matter how good their track record in calling things correctly; they are always wondering what's next and which surprises are yet to come.

Getting Better at Diagnosing

No one excels at diagnostics—but we can all get better.

The first thing to be is *curious*. Good strategists are never complacent, no matter how good their track record in calling things correctly; they are always wondering what's next and which surprises are yet to come. This requires a daily habit of probing, questioning, and being in a state of wonder and bemusement. When something is working really well—find out why. When things have worked out surprisingly badly, always figure out—what really went wrong here? What was not foreseen?

Next, get *out and about*. In my leadership program, Fast Forward, we call this listening to *the sound of the river*—based on an Irish proverb: "If you want to catch fish, listen to the sound of the river." The river is where the customers and suppliers and frontline employees are. As we climb up the ladder, we tend to live in the treetops, high above the river, from where its sound is just a distant hum. I have said the same thing to every CEO I have ever advised—get down there, walk around, chat, ask questions. Develop your own feeling about what's happening—don't rely on others or on heavily edited market reports. Stay in touch.

Third, *mix it up*. Team diversity is really, really important. If you have a team that's trying to make sense of the present and future, make sure you get a great mix of personalities, experiences, perspectives, ages, and backgrounds. If you all look the same, sound the same, and think the same, guess what? You will all conclude exactly the same things—and probably miss a whole bunch of issues.

Fourth, watch the *data* very keenly. We have more data available to us now than any time in human history. We must use it. We can use the numbers to discern patterns and make more nuanced guesses. Is this a general trend, or is it only in local pockets? Why is there more activity at that time of day? Is the rate of change constant, or is it increasing? Which surprising products are getting a significant share of customer spend? What do our best customers always buy? The people who pore over those statistics can tell you a lot, as can machine-learning algorithms. Give them a loud voice.

Fifth, catch your own *biases* whenever you can. Good diagnosticians are not driven by what they wish will happen, nor are they affected by what they believe to be true. We have to put our own sentiments to one side and study the situation dispassionately. I, for example, love the roar of my car's combustion engine—but I must not let that blind me to the coming wave of electric vehicles. I love old-fashioned bookshops and support them to the hilt—but that does not mean I can look away from the reality of the click-click convenience that Amazon brings.

Sixth, be *reflective* and introspective, and never absolutely certain. Be self-critical, not super sure of your ground. Your ego has no place in diagnosing—it will just prevent you from seeing important things. Don't come to the table wedded to any particular agenda; otherwise, confirmation bias will be your only discovery process.

Last, always keep an eye on *youth culture*—no matter how old you are. The young are the vanguard of what's coming. If you want to spot a consumer trend before it's big, you will never see it in the middle-aged or the elderly—those folks have settled into deep grooves. Spend time with people much younger than yourself and figure out their ways, without judgment or admonition. And please, for heaven's sake, when with the young, never talk about yourself back in the good ol' days . . . just watch and listen and quietly sketch a picture of what's about to change.

I referred to professors Kay and King in the last chapter, and they have more inspiration for us about facing uncertainty. They tell us that "emperors, explorers, and presidents" have all made big decisions without having a full understanding of what was going on. So must we!

The Heart of the Matter

If you have been doing a good job as a curious strategist who doesn't stop finding out, doesn't stop probing, doesn't rest on your laurels, then here's the good news: you probably *already* know a great deal more than you think you do.

I find this often when I meet management teams who are ready to start diagnosing. The boss often feels a fresh market survey is needed; but unless the team has been doing its work with its eyes closed, the essential state of play is already known. A team of diverse talents with a curious bent and lots of time spent on the frontlines and in poring over numbers will be able to call the big trends. The threads just need to be drawn out gently and then pulled together.

What matters is the ability to turn all the opinions, conjectures, and data into an actionable diagnosis—ideally a clear statement on a single slide. Remember, the point of the diagnosis is not to cover every possibility and build every scenario—it is to agree on our best understanding of the challenge, and then frame it in a way that is clear and concise.

Richard Rumelt, who was one of the first to spell out the importance of a good diagnosis, told us that it is but an educated guess—a way of replacing "overwhelming complexity" with "a simpler story" in order to focus on what's really crucial.

So there you are with your team, faced with a mountain of data and an ocean of opinions. Every piece of information seems important; every point of view feels valid. What are you going to do?

Before you begin, please understand: most of what you will consider is just noise, not a signal.

The excellent strategist is the one who can find the essential signal amidst the deafening noise. In any given situation these days, there is an overwhelming amount of information available. There are a multitude of forces at play. We can spend days constructing the SWOT and PEST charts of yore; we can commission study after tedious study. Or we can just pay deep, focused attention. Not every thing matters; not every sound must be studied.

Media companies the world over, for example, have endured a very difficult decade. Many previously successful ones have gone out of business. If you sit down with media executives to discuss their many challenges, a long list will emerge: falling revenues; migrating customers; too much overhead; regulatory frictions; inability to charge for content; fake-news pandemics. Noise; noise; noise.

Where's the signal in the noise? Old-world media houses are facing the challenge of *relevance*. Their consumers have changed right under their noses, using their ever-present devices to consume news and entertainment in ever more surprising ways, as an undying stream, rather than episodically. As media companies' ability to attract eyeballs has faltered, so has their ability to attract advertisers. So what's the way forward? It is not in sinking more investment in the legacy businesses or shedding talent even faster or fiddling with content scheduling; it is in getting real about the world we actually live in today. It is in finding the few remaining advantages an old-media company might still possess (a reputation for truth or for generating unique, desirable content, perhaps) and using those

---

The strategist is the one who can get to the heart of the matter quickly and frame the challenge succinctly.

---

strategic assets to build a new business that is able to dance to the new music—whose key notes are mobile-first, always on, and in tune with youth culture. The real challenge is to rethink and reorganize for a radically different world.

The strategist is the one who can get to the heart of the matter quickly and frame the challenge succinctly. Long lists may be comprehensive, but they do not spur action. They encourage lethargy. To win the game that's ahead of us, we must also *become* something.

What Do We Need to Become?

Richard Rumelt tells us that our diagnosis should also suggest "a domain of action"—and that's absolutely right. We are not trying to make intellectual predictions or play guessing games—we are trying to understand what we must *do and become* in order to succeed.

Let's take Apple, the world's most successful business of the past decade or so. What do you think Apple's diagnosis of the future might have been around the time the first iPhone was launched? Certainly, Apple executives could see the importance of a mobile device—cellphones had been around for a while. But an easy-to-use handheld computing device was a different matter. Nokia and BlackBerry ruled the roost at the time, but their interfaces were clunky and awkward (remember pressing a key three times to get the letter of the alphabet you wanted or pushing knobs to move cursors awkwardly on the screen?).

When the first iPhone came out, it was a revelation. Elegant, simple, and easy to use. You could carry your music on it; browse the web on it; take photos on it. But it was still basically a phone. The real changes came in later iterations: the app store opened up a new universe of functionality; larger screens made it possible to do more complicated things with the device; more power-ful chips turned it into something capable of advanced computing; better cameras caused an explosion in photo snapping and video shooting.

Google quickly spotted the potential, released the Android mobile operating system for free to smart-phone manufacturers—and the global revolution in mobile computing was underway.

As I write this, there are nearly four billion humans using smartphones in the world. Most of us cannot do without these devices (think about how *you* behave when you've forgotten your phone behind). They are our cameras, our computers, our maps, our music players, our encyclopedias, our libraries, our wallets, our banks, our news feeds, our TV screens, our filing cabinets—and our social lives.

None of this happened overnight, though—and I bet no one at Apple or Google predicted it would turn out quite this way a decade ago. What they have both been very good at is framing the challenge, and then acting on it and learning as they go. The first iPhones and Android devices were just trial balloons. How the ecosystem of users and suppliers responded is what led to the next steps.

So if you're Team Apple a few years ago, how do you frame the challenge? To be clear, I was not in the room with them! But I was watching the smartphone phe-nomenon and Apple very closely at the time. In April 2010 I wrote in my regular newspaper column:

The future of your business lies in the palm of your hand. No, I

haven't suddenly developed a
superstitious belief in palmistry.
I am referring to the thing that
is in your palm most of the time
these days: your mobile phone.
The cellphone, by mutating into
the smartphone, has come of
age. When combined with the
widespread advent of broad-
band connectivity, it is going
to whack every industry on
the head.

Here's one way Apple might have framed that diagnosis for themselves:

APPLE'S DIAGNOSIS (C. 2010)

Connected devices will rule the world, and the only viable place for
Apple to make money is at the top end of the market.

That's how I think it got framed. Take a closer look.
That diagnosis has two parts. First, there's the importance given to connected devices. Given the early popularity of the iPhone (and, a little later, its larger cousin,
the iPad) and the insertion of the devices into everyone's lives, that one was perhaps easier to predict—it
was unfurling in real time anyway.

The second part is more interesting. Apple also
predicted the commoditization of the handset and
the operating system. Very good phones were being
churned out of China by the container-load, and Google

was busy giving them all the exact same operating system for free. Product differentiation would be very difficult, and margins would collapse to almost nothing. Unless you were Apple.

Apple had a brand that said premium; it had a history of emphasizing elegance in design (founder Steve Jobs's withering criticism of his rival Bill Gates's Microsoft was that they had "no taste"); and it controlled both its own hardware and software. That gave it the platform with which to pitch its tent at the top end of the market: expensive and aspirational. So as rivals began trumpeting new features, functions, and ever-falling prices, Apple set about doing the opposite: quietly pitching its devices as luxury products. More on how it did this later; my aim at this stage is to show you the prescience in the gaze.

That diagnosis, please note, was not what Google saw—looking at the exact same situation. The first part—that everyone on earth would soon carry a connected device on them and use it for a multitude of things every day—was obvious to Google as well. But unlike Apple, it was not interested in making its own devices or commanding big margins on them.

Google's economic engine is different: it aims to get everyone's attention by being on every device in a bewildering array of forms—a search engine, a map app, an email client, a photo library, a web browser, a video platform, a cloud storage service, and dozens more— because it makes money by packaging you, the user, as a data profile and selling you to advertisers. The richer and more comprehensive the data, the greater Google's power over advertisers. So Google had to get your eyeballs on its digital services by making them enormously useful in your life.

GOOGLE'S DIAGNOSIS (C. 2010)

DIAGNOSIS	Connected devices will rule the world, and Google must be on all of them and attract all of the world's attention.

So Apple will charge you, the user, an eye-watering amount for its products; Google will mostly give them to you for free. Both companies are very successful; both responded to the same environment; but both framed the challenge differently. One set out to be aspirational; the other to be ubiquitous.

Both companies were now poised for action. The next step in their strategies suggested itself—the positioning. And that's the next chapter in this book.

What's Really Going on Here?

Let's conclude.

How do you go about getting the first part of the strategy four-stepper dance done?

Remember what you're trying to do is answer this question: "What's *really* going on here?"

To this question there is no correct answer. There are only educated guesses.

To make these guesses, you need to tap into a bunch of people. No CEO, strategy guru, forecasting wonk, or AI-powered algorithm can do it alone. We are all prone to biases (even the algorithms); and we all have only a limited number of lenses at our disposal.

So you, the organizational strategist, must assemble a team that has multiple perspectives and brings different skills and experiences to the game. This team must off-load all its data, studies, opinions, evidence, and anecdotes on the table. Now you must sift through the mess together, pick out what seems crucial, and gain consensus on the final choices.

Next, you must summarize the key challenge—and the domain of action it suggests.

Finally, you must find the words to put it all in a couple of powerful sentences, or a couple of paragraphs at most.

Step back, gaze upon your work, see if it gives you the confidence to move to the next stage in the dance. And please don't look for perfect confidence; how right or wrong your diagnosis is will be discovered later. You will amend it as you go. All you need to do now is gather yourself as the music changes, and then consider the next step—your *positioning*.

SECOND STEP:
TAKE YOUR POSITION

*"The best use of
military power is to use
superior positioning
to force a surrender."*
—SUN TZU

One of the first people to talk about positioning as being at the heart of strategy was Professor Michael Porter. I had the privilege of introducing him to an audience of Kenyan leaders a few years back, and I spent some very instructive hours in his company.

One of Michael Porter's most important contributions came in a landmark essay for the *Harvard Business Review* in 1996. It was entitled "What Is Strategy?"—an odd question, you might think, for something that has seemingly been well understood for centuries. Not so. As I have indicated earlier in this book, the field of strategy can be an extremely complex and confusing one, even for those who profess to be experts in it. Porter, with his customary lucidity, pointed out that there is an important distinction to be made between *strategy* and *operational effectiveness*.

The strategic winner is the one who routinely sinks birdies and eagles, not the one who keeps par.

The words still ring in my mind: Strategy is not about doing things better; it's about doing things differently. It's about delineating a territory in which you are unique. It's about making difficult choices, not about being more efficient. Difference is the key to strategy.

This is a great lesson for the many companies in the world that are obsessed with "benchmarking" and adopting "best practice." Making operational improvements on a continuous basis may be necessary, but it is never going to be sufficient.

The imitation game is a small-player's game; the big fish aren't in the same pond as you. They're out there controlling the big blue oceans.

Competitive advantage is about difference, about scarcity, about uniqueness. It is about doing things that others cannot do, or about doing things that others *can* do, but doing them in your own special (and valuable) way. It is *not* about having a list of achievements or simply focusing on the things that are "par for the course" in your market.

The strategic winner is the one who routinely sinks birdies and eagles, not the one who keeps par.

Don't Be Competitive, Be Distinctive

I once saw a leading, award-winning company answer the question, "What is your competitive advantage?" with the following list:

One, we have vast local and international experience.
Two, we have invested in very efficient processes.
Three, we offer superior customer service.
Four, we have well-qualified staff at all levels.
Five, we have been awarded several certifications, such as ISO 9001:2000.

Feel free to roll your eyes with me here.

Not *one* of those things constitutes a competitive advantage in itself.

Experience, no matter how vast and lengthy, is by itself nothing, unless it helps you lower costs, understand customers, or motivate staff in ways that other companies cannot.

Customer service is by itself nothing, unless it is remarkably better than that provided by your rivals and greatly valued by customers.

Processes, similarly, must add great value to suppliers or customers in ways that competitors' processes simply cannot.

Well-qualified staff? Really? This is an achievement? Do your competitors work with unqualified bumpkins?

And certifications? Don't even go there. Those awards that we all seem to be so proud of are widely available to all, and they rarely mean a damn thing to customers. There is nothing at all strategic there.

You do not outpace competitors by doing things a little better than them; you beat them by doing things in a way that they simply cannot match. For the moment.

Indeed, modern-day strategy does not emphasize things you can hold and touch, like plants and equipment and servers and vehicles: it focuses on the things that you can't see. A company's reputation or standing with the outside world; its emotional bond with its key customers; the way in which it motivates its people to do the extraordinary—those are the things that competitors can't mimic or replicate.

Think about it: your IT system—even if it's top-notch and world-class—is, in itself, nothing. Or rather, nothing strategic. Sure, it helps you work better and manage yourself more efficiently (maybe), but nothing stops your competitors from buying that exact same system and configuring it in the exact same way you do. In fact, there will be an army of vendors, trainers, and consultants available to help them do exactly that.

But your IT system can be a cog in a bigger machine that does deliver great strategy—if it assembles data, enriches it through analysis, and passes it on to highly motivated people who use it to very good effect in making strategic decisions and serving customers better.

It is in those intangible relationships that strategy lies; it's in why your people work better, why your processes flow better, and why your customers love you.

Competitive Advantage and Distinctive Capabilities

Great strategy is built on having a competitive edge. The professors will tell you: strategy is about the systematic development and exploitation of competitive advantage.

Richard Rumelt simplifies competitive advantage best: if you can take business away from competitors at a profit, you have a competitive advantage. There must be something you're doing that creates a good result, something that pleases customers more than your competitors' efforts do.

Please note that this does not refer to taking business from rivals by cutting prices to the bone or by making your products ruinously attractive or by engaging in corrupt contracts—anyone can do that. You have to be able to take business away *and* make money. Equally, your competitive advantage has to survive for a period of time. If it evaporates quickly—if your competitors can match what you do with ease—then it's not much of an advantage.

Competitive advantage is founded on distinctive capabilities—things your organization does that are truly special, that your competitors wish they had, that generate love for your offerings. Let's look at some.

Coca-Cola is one of the world's most consistently profitable companies. It just sells sugared water, yet many would-be rivals over many decades have failed to take market share. Only PepsiCo has come close. Most wannabes come and bash their heads against an unyielding wall and fall away, bloodied. Why should this be? There are two truly distinctive capabilities at play here: brand power and distribution strength. Coca-Cola invests massively in these two capabilities; indeed, if you visit the company's many regional HQs, you will find there is little else its key staffers do (the messy business of actually producing soft drinks is mostly left for franchisee bottlers to manage).

People at Coke have huge budgets to keep two parts of the soft-drinks game protected: brand and distribution. One set of people engages incessantly with advertising campaigns, brand visibility, and youth culture; another set is obsessed with helping the bottlers get product to market—all markets.

That's why every kid knows Coca-Cola and its many cousin products; and that's why you are more likely to find a Coke in remote parts of this globe than you are to find drinkable water.

Coca-Cola has, of course, a lot more going for it. Very talented people? Tick. State-of-the-art information technology? Tick. Very efficient processes? Tick. But that's not where the magic is. Those are just the support acts. What's special about Coke, what it has that others find very difficult to replicate, is enormous brand and distribution power.

That's true strategic focus, and it has served the company well for more than a century.

Think about other dominant firms, and you will see that their strategic strength comes from distinctive capabilities. For Apple, it's the ease of use and product elegance that are difficult to match. For Porsche, it's all about brand positioning and product distinction. For Netflix, it's friction-free user experience and massive investment in content creation and procurement.

When Michael Porter was in Nairobi, he explained to his enrapt audience an essential point: competitive advantage, said the famous don, is not about *what* you do; it's about *how* you do it. All the winning companies are not just taking a desirable position; they are working systematically to develop it.

Here's an example I remember well.

"You can become very poor making shoes, or you can become very rich making shoes," said Professor Porter. He was explaining the phenomenon of international competition. Shoemaking in the modern era would not, on the face of it, seem to have much going for it. A low-tech industry, a boring product—not something to stake your national fortune on. Unless you happen to be Italian. Those who run shoe companies in Italy, Porter revealed, are rich enough to live in castles and

own private planes. Those who work as ordinary labor-
ers in that industry earn top-notch wages.

In Italy, shoemaking is serious business. In many
other countries, it is an uninteresting pastime churning
out low-cost footwear made by low-paid armies.

In Italy, shoemaking is serious business. In many other countries, it is an uninteresting pastime churning out low-cost footwear made by low-paid armies. What makes Italy different?

What makes Italy different? The talent of its designers, for one thing. The tremendous investment in building exclusive global brands, for another. Not to forget

the carefully crafted softness of the leather itself. All of that means that Italy can sell shoes to the world for many hundreds of dollars per pair—and do it year after year.

The trick lies in the uniqueness of the "how."

Types of Distinctive Capabilities

Can we organize these distinctive capabilities—special ways of doing things that lead to competitive advantage—in archetypes?

I have worked with organizations of all shapes and sizes and on multiple continents, and I offer the following set of general categories:

» *Brand power*: As we saw from the Coca-Cola example, a great brand can bestow immense strategic power by providing a unique emotional connection with a set of customers—a reputation that is difficult for others to build up quickly. But remember that brand is not fluff; it is a promise that must actually be delivered, year after year after year.

» *Captive resources*: Some organizations have special resources that they can hold on to and prevent others from accessing. A unique talent pool, with long-term commitments to the organization, might be one. Special knowledge or intellectual property, built over time and unavailable to others, might be another. Licenses granted by governments to run an activity exclusively can provide a different type of captive resource (albeit a frequently misused one).

» *Unique processes*: Firms often come up with special ways of running things, and they can stand out in terms of operational excellence. Distinctively configured manufacturing facilities; outstanding organizational techniques; superior workflow arrangements—all of these can yield advantage in the market by allowing their practitioners to improve quality or lower costs. *But* in today's world of ever-faster best-practice dissemination and relentless benchmarking, it is rare for this type of advantage to be truly distinctive or last very long.

» *Special relationships*: This set of capabilities is often the least appreciated—yet it can be the most powerful. Many outstanding organizations make unusual human connections—with their workforce, with suppliers, with distributors, with investors. If these relationships are nurtured and protected (and ethical), they can provide an enduring source of advantage—and one that is very difficult to emulate. The set of behavioral relationships we call culture, for example, is hugely important in giving distinction to organizations (more on this later, in chapter 9).

» *Leadership*: Does the way organizations are led bestow strategic power? I believe it does—so much so that I paused my career as a strategy guy to focus more on leadership. Leadership can be an accelerant for strategy—but it can also be a huge obstacle. Many a strategy has failed to get off the ground because of the resistance or shortsightedness of its leaders. And many a strategy has hit the heights because of the vision and single-minded dedication of its leadership cadres. As you think about this factor in your organization, please note that this is not about the larger-than-life charismatic leader of popular myth. It is about creating enlightened leadership capacity as an ongoing capability, at all levels.

A caveat is important here. I offer the list above not so that you can trawl through the categories at your next leadership retreat and try to build some or all of those capabilities for your organization. That's not how it works. Don't start filling a flip chart with capabilities you *wish* to have. The best capabilities evolve over time, often serendipitously.

Coca-Cola did not set out to become one of the world's leading brands at its birth in Atlanta in the US; it understood the power of branding as its product began gaining popularity and traversing the country and the globe.

Success also comes from deep wisdoms about local context. East African Breweries figured out decades ago that external relationships were really important for a giant corporation in Africa. Sustained market power would only come from *ecosystem* thinking in its strategy—nurturing deep and long-lived partnerships with a wide range of players, from "grain to glass." It has carefully made itself the nexus of a web of relationships—with farmers, agricultural research organizations, retailers and bars, supply chain partners, and local communities. Success is therefore shared and mutual. This way of thinking—of going beyond the boundaries of the organization—gives it greater strength against competitors, better leeway with regulators, and an ability to withstand the unexpected, such as the coronavirus pandemic.

What should you do with the list of categories above? Look through it; know that these are the activities that are the building blocks of strategic advantage. Look around at market leaders and see if you can understand which distinctive capabilities they are leaning on. Look inward, and understand where your organization's uniqueness comes from—where does your particular power lie? Is this something you can deepen and make more of? Are there capabilities you have that are not particularly distinctive—but that could be made so? Can you start a process of deepening?

Should you look through my list and see *nothing* that rings a bell for your organization, no real source of distinction, then good luck—you'll need it. Without any

distinctive capabilities, you can only play for mediocrity and be one of the crowd of the also-present.

Be the Mostest

Capabilities only matter if they are distinctive. To be
decent at anything is all very well, but it isn't strategic.
Even to be equivalent to market leaders is not something to get particularly excited about. If four or five
firms in the market have equally good brands or similarly excellent products, this is an achievement, sure—
but it's not exceptional. It just means there will be a
bunch of players always jockeying for top spot. One of
them has to break away with something unusual.

Author Bill Taylor frames this nicely as a question:
"What are you the most of?" In a 2018 interview, he
explained that you should not be happy to be a little
better at some things than everybody else. The goal is
not to be "the best at what lots of others already do." It
is "to be the only one who does what you do."

Nicely put. We have to think hard about what we are,
or can be, the "most of."

Some companies are the "most of" fast and friction-
less user experience.

Some are the most of distribution-chain efficiency.

Some are the most of employee experience, which
simply causes their people to give more.

Some are the most of brand connection and
recognition.

If those "mosts" deliver results in the market because
they matter to customers, then they are distinctive

capabilities. Most organizations, however, are not the most of anything. They are mostly the "just enough of" everything. And therefore they fail at strategy.

So a sobering question for your next strategy session is: "What are we the most of?"

Strategists Say No Often

If you want to be more strategic in life, I'm about to write down a sentence that may be one of the most important things you will ever read. It was said by Warren Buffett, and here it is:

> The difference between success-
> ful people and really successful
> people is that really success-
> ful people say no to almost
> everything.

If that sentence immediately made perfect sense to you, then you are probably already en route to genuine success. If not, some clarification is needed.

Saying no is not something many people teach us. In fact, we are taught the opposite: to say yes a lot. To embrace opportunities as they arise; to be agreeable; to be positive and optimistic; to attempt many things; to try to have it all.

All those are mistakes that await you like camouflaged pits in your path.

But wait. Mr. Buffett did not refer to unsuccessful people; he pointed out that the habit of saying no differentiates successful and *really* successful people. In other words, you can be successful by saying yes a lot of the time. You can engage in multiple ventures; try many things; add many hustles; keep many people happy. Your life will look pretty good, and you may be quite pleased with it.

But real success? That's different. That's deep; it's focused; it has clear boundaries. It's almost manic in saying no. To almost everything.

Why should this be so? For the very simple reason that we are given very limited time on this earth. We do not have the luxury of pulling it all off—doing all the things we want to do; running down all the paths that look interesting; spending time with every person who resonates or seems intriguing; visiting every part of the world; keeping every friend or family member happy; trying everything out; playing every possible role in our lives.

That's why we have to choose. Choose carefully, choose brutally. And that means saying no. A lot.

Trying a lot of stuff out, being curious, being ready to give many things a go is a plan—when you're young. After a certain age, however, you had better get your no muscle working—otherwise you will never go deep on any one thing.

Saying no to most things is tough; make no mistake. It can cause offense with people who are demanding your time or your resources. It can lead to many regrets, if what you said no to turned out actually to be a great thing for someone else. It can make you feel like a nay-sayer and a wet blanket. So you need some steel in you in order to say no often. It's not for those who aim to please, or those without any clear sense of purpose.

And that's exactly why very few people are really successful. They've been saying yes all their lives—to too many people, too many projects, too many distractions. They've made too many commitments. They've swum on the surface of achievement and never encountered the depths.

Warren Buffett has further advice for you, in three steps. First, write down a list of your top twenty-five career goals. Second, circle the five most important goals that connect deeply with you, that feel nonnegotiable. So far, so good? But here's the kicker: third, cross off the other twenty goals you have listed. Delete them. Expunge them. From now on, just focus on the top five.

It's that brutal. Why? Because expending any energy on the "next twenty" will come at the cost of the "top five."

That's true in business strategy; it's true in friendships and relationships; it's true in managing the multiplicity of things that make up a life. Focus. Say no to distraction; to overwork; to seduction; and to flitting around, pleasing everyone by doing everything and achieving nothing.

This does not mean you have to become a sourpuss who's instinctively negative about everything. You can be completely honest and courteous about how you say no. It's not something you have to be ashamed of—it's simple prioritization. No one should set your life's agendas for you. That's your call, your right, your prerogative. Hang out with people who understand and support your priorities, not those who try to thwart them for their own ends.

And yet, always keep a small part of yourself open to new things, no matter how focused you are in your life. Leave a window open for serendipity.

Say no to distraction; to overwork; to seduction; and to flitting around, pleasing everyone by doing everything and achieving nothing.

At the end of the day, however, only a few things are worth your time. Give those things your best time, not the same amount of time you give everything else. Then watch the best of your life come to life.

That's an important life lesson, but it's also a vital lesson in strategy. To understand this, consider the challenge of saying no from a different angle. Let's go from Buffett, the man, to buffet, the meal.

Remember the lavish buffet? The coronavirus put the skids on that excellent phenomenon in food-sharing—the enticing range of sumptuous dishes: starters, salads, mains, desserts.

I was very sad to see the buffet lose its ubiquity. Not because I indulged excessively, I hasten to add, but because it gave me a near-foolproof method of spotting natural strategists. Buffets allowed me to clock a proper strategist long before we did any strategy work together. All I needed was for us to have a meal together—but that meal needed to involve a buffet table.

The nonstrategist does this at the buffet: he or she starts piling various dishes on the plate quickly, without rhyme or reason, in large quantities, trying pretty much everything out.

And here's what the natural strategist does: first a slow recce of the whole buffet, noting everything that's on offer; and then a focused, narrow selection of dishes that actually go together or that offer the promise of superior look and taste.

The strategist chooses, in other words. Everyone else just piles it on.

Why do most people fail to discriminate when confronted with an all-you-can-eat buffet, though? I am not referring here to relatively impoverished people who encounter their first chance to eat well at a buffet. We might forgive them for grabbing their chance. But those are not the only people engorging themselves haphazardly and injudiciously at smorgasbords all over the world. Even well-to-do, seasoned diners can be seen overdoing it. Why so?

There are two reasons. First, there is the fallacy of thinking that if something is paid for, it must be exploited to the full. Second, there is the misjudgment that everything that is available must be taken. Most people think exactly like that. Strategists, however, do not.

If you have paid for the buffet, that act is done. It's in the past. It's a cost that's been incurred. It is now sunk. What matters now is what comes next. The buffet can now be enjoyed—or suffered. The pleasure of gluttony, if it exists at all, is only momentary. The body cannot take that kind of excess, and pain and discomfort soon follow. Many people seem to behave even more extremely when someone else has paid for the buffet. Witness the stampedes for food we see at some weddings . . .

A wide-ranging repast, equally, is not a license for excess. Feasts have a large selection not so that you try every damn thing that's before you; the range is there to give you choices. You can look at every dish, consider its merits, and then decide what really matters to you and choose accordingly.

Doing well at strategy, folks, is exactly the same as doing well at the buffet table. It requires three disciplines. First, genuine *focus*—making real choices from among competing alternatives. Really successful businesses do not try to make every possible offering or pitch for every possible customer. They go narrow and go deep. They offer genuinely distinctive value to their chosen markets.

Second, *harmony*. Strategy is a symphony, not a medley; it's a novel, not a collection of disparate tales.

A proper strategy is coherent. Its parts fit together, and every element benefits from the others.

And the third discipline of the natural strategist? That of *foresight*. Good strategists are forward-looking; they go beyond the current situation and create a game plan for a future that's not quite visible yet. They look up, and they look ahead.

Just as the wise buffet visitor considers the consequences of overdoing the feast, the wise strategist looks beyond the temptations and traps of the present and pitches for something that is selective, sustainable, and farsighted, not that which is fixated on immediate, illusory gain.

So I used to advise: if you're a board looking for a CEO with a good strategic brain, or a CEO looking for a natural strategist to join your team, ask the candidate to prepare a presentation on strategy for your organization, by all means. But also take the candidate out for lunch. Just make sure it's a buffet, and watch what happens next very carefully . . .

All Things to All People = Fail

> *We are going for the consumer market, we are going to the business market, we are going to the low end, we are going to the developing markets.*

That was said in 2010 by Nokia's then CEO, Olli-Pekka Kallasvuo. I immediately thought, *Uh oh, Nokia—bad idea. Very bad idea*, and wrote a newspaper column to that effect.

He left the job within a matter of months. Nokia's subsequent meltdown is a matter of record. During this CEO's tenure, Nokia lost over $60 billion in market value since Apple had introduced its iPhone in 2007.

Mr. Kallasvuo effectively said in that interview that he wanted the company to be all things to all consumers. The mobile-phone giant, he said, intended to aim for high-end and low-end handset markets simultaneously. It wanted to cater to both the business market and the consumer market. It wanted to dominate both developing and advanced-economy markets.

Whenever I hear a CEO spouting that kind of ambition, alarm bells start going off in my head. All my experience as a strategy advisor suggests a simple truth: the company that tries to be all things to all customers in all markets fails.

The essential point is this: customers respond to products that match their specific needs. When faced with worthy rivals, competitive advantage is a devilishly difficult thing for any company. Achieving it for one set of customers in one socioeconomic group is hard enough; achieving it for all is all but impossible. Customers soon vote with their feet on the weaker segments and products.

Strategic success comes from distinctive capabilities applied in carefully chosen market segments—not from mediocre capabilities applied across the board.

Now let's add a different flavor to the all-things-to-all-people pot.

Tony Fernandes is the flamboyant owner of AirAsia. Vijay Mallya was the flamboyant owner of Kingfisher Airlines. Both owners seemed to model themselves on the original flamboyant airline owner, Richard Branson of Virgin.

AirAsia was very successful for a long time. Based in Malaysia, it introduced budget air travel to the Southeast Asia market. It enjoyed rising revenues and net income for many years, a feat most other airlines have not managed to pull off.

Kingfisher was never successful. It almost never made a profit since listing in India in 2006, and it finally gave up the ghost in 2012, owing its staff, lenders, airports, and suppliers huge amounts.

In a 2013 interview, Tony said that he had warned Vijay that airlines are a very tough business, one in which a fortune can be lost very quickly. The key, he said, was to have focus, which Kingfisher patently lacked. It was trying to be low-cost and premium, short-haul and long-haul, all at the same time. It was, in his telling, a "bad biryani."

Too many ingredients, too many target customer segments, too many cooks led by a head chef who wanted to do it all, and who had many other dishes on the boil at the same time (Vijay also ran a brewery and a cricket team franchise).

It doesn't work. Kingfisher tried to be the airline of choice to the premium traveler; it tried to compete head-on with low-cost carriers, despite having a huge cost base set up for premium travel; and it tried to win at home as well as abroad, without doing either particularly well. It was a beer brand as well as an airline brand.

Biryanis, as any chef and gourmet will tell you, are not at all easy to make. They require a great recipe; superior ingredients; painstaking attention. I have probably not eaten more than a handful of truly great

---

I have probably not eaten more than a handful of truly great biryanis in a lifetime of trying them out. I have also not personally encountered more than a handful of truly great businesses. Coincidence?

---

biryanis in a lifetime of trying them out. I have also not personally encountered more than a handful of truly great businesses. Coincidence?

To prevent your business from becoming a bad biryani, remember the following: superior ingredients, but not too many; a tried-and-tested recipe, ideally generations old; no tampering with the essentials; and pride in a high standard that you will not allow to be lowered. Then perhaps you, too, can create a masterpiece.

Sadly, Tony Fernandes did not seem to follow his own excellent advice. He, too, began dabbling in multiple airline routes and models; he, too, began stretching out into myriad unrelated ventures, such as buying an English football team and a Formula One racing team. The football team was relegated; the F1 team collapsed into administration.

In 2020, the year all airlines were grounded by the COVID-19 global pandemic, AirAsia also ran into serious trouble, saddled with debt and facing severe liquidity constraints. The *Financial Times* reported in October 2020: "Mr. Fernandes is now concentrating on the airline after years of high-profile forays into different sectors. 'AirAsia is the most important baby to me so that's where most of my focus will be,' he said."

Ahem. Welcome back to a focused strategy, Tony.

But wait, you say. Let's look beyond buffets and biryanis. These days the tech giants have changed those rules, haven't they? They are engaged in all sorts of adjacent ventures. Apple makes hardware and software, sells music, offers payment systems, runs a TV service, and packages news. Amazon is not just an e-commerce giant in all product categories; it also dominates cloud services, runs music and video-streaming services, and is busy developing a robotics capability. Google was once just a search engine but is today one of the two giants in online advertising as well as a leader in software, mapping, and video streaming. Safaricom is not just a calls 'n' data vendor—it dominates the payments landscape in Kenya.

Indeed true. When your operations run on bits and bytes, some of the old boundaries melt away. Netflix, for instance, was able to expand its global footprint to 160 countries overnight—by flicking a switch. Imagine an old-media company attempting the same: painstaking market research, talent acquisition, equipment setup and regulatory compliance, country by country.

Digital technology allows many businesses to transcend old-world boundaries. And yet. Look carefully, and the timeless lesson of distinctive capabilities still holds. It was not a huge stretch for Amazon to become not just an online bookseller but an e-commerce behemoth—the skill sets and infrastructure were identical and just needed to scale. Its market-leading Amazon Web Services grew directly out of the need to have extremely stable and robust cloud storage for its own exploding e-commerce business, initially—but the early learnings in going vertical allowed it to go horizontal as well and extend this expertise and capacity to other companies.

Apple may make brilliant handsets—but it has never come close to matching Google in maps. Apple now has video-streaming products—but it remains far behind global giant Netflix, which has corralled much of the expertise and know-how needed for the very distinct entertainment sector. Audio-focused Spotify smacks Apple—usually the user-interface king—in music-streaming user experience all day long.

It should also be noted that these new-world organizations are adding fresh elements that are complementary to their core businesses. Apple is adding new services like payments and gaming and news because it already has a huge captive base of iOS devices in the world and is moving itself toward a recurring revenue and subscriptions model. The heart of Amazon is still in taking over world retail, and all its best new moves are building on its existing assets or capabilities. Safaricom deployed all its key assets—people and network—to make M-PESA succeed alongside its traditional telco business.

So the rapidly growing digital substrate may be uprooting old fences and changing the scope of the multibusiness firm, but the essential lesson remains the same. Don't become a bad biryani by throwing too many ingredients into the pot. The advice of Michael Porter should never be forgotten: to compete across markets, you first have to be competitive in each of them.

Defining Your Positioning

Now we can conclude with how you define your positioning. So far in this chapter, I hope certain essential truths about taking positions have emerged:

- » That superior positioning is essentially about difference, not equivalence.
- » That the difference must matter to the market the organization serves.

»   That the difference must be scarce and difficult for others to copy.

»   That the difference must keep evolving with its market.

»   That the difference cannot be wished into existence; it must come from repeated activities that build unique capabilities over time.

»   That saying no is an essential habit of the strategist.

»   That focus is the essence of good strategy—only doing the things you can be outstanding at doing.

Now we are ready to define our positioning—clearly and concisely.

The best way to do this comes from Roger Martin, introduced earlier. His book *Playing to Win* (written with P&G's legendary former CEO, A. G. Lafley) zooms in on the two essential questions of positioning:

1. Where to play.
2. How to win.

The first question asks us to make choices about our strategic territory: the products or services we can be best at offering and the market segments, geographies, or demographic groups we can make our own.

The second asks about the sources of our advantage— how will we excel and be better than our rivals?

Here's my take on how some leading organizations have answered those two essential questions of positioning: *where* and *how*.

Remember Italian shoes? The best footwear brands from that country have made active choices. Their "where" is the global luxury goods market; their "how" is through superior design, quality, and branding.

Look at what they're *not* doing: They're not competing in the mass market for shoes—which is a huge market—and they're not competing on price.

Where does Coca-Cola play? Literally everywhere in the world. How does it win? Through product desirability fed by incessant branding activity and consistent availability.

Netflix? Where? All over the earth, on all types of devices. How? By emphasizing smooth and easy user experience, and by having the most comprehensive content library.

Safaricom straddles Kenya like a behemoth (and is now trying to make major inroads beyond its borders), but it uses its brand and footprint to play in the very lucrative financial payments segment, not just SIM cards and routers.

More systematically, let's look at Apple in recent years. What positioning were they taking?

APPLE'S POSITIONING, 2010–20

Where We Play	Where: aspirational, top of the market Where: vertical integration of chips, hardware, software, stores Where: whichever device(s) you prefer Where: services, recurring revenues
How We Win	How: high-touch, high-visibility brand How: the easiest to use How: seamless across devices How: we sell art, not just technology

I hope you can see the clarity of the positioning:

Apple wanted to sell highly aspirational products across the world, but without ever looking like a mass-market player.

It wanted to have tight control over the user experience, and so it moved upstream into chip-making and downstream into retailing.

It wanted simplicity to be the hallmark of the user experience (have you ever read an Apple manual?).

It wanted to offer seamless connections between its many devices (your stuff floats from your iPhone to your Mac to your iPad to your Apple Watch to your TV without any glitches).

And it wanted to uniquely be the company that emphasizes the artistry and elegance of its products and experiences.

Apple's huge achievement is to be able to sell a massive number of expensive devices at enormous scale. As Professor Scott Galloway often puts it in his podcasts: the iPhone sells Toyota volumes with Ferrari margins! This is not a feat many have pulled off in business history. Apple became the world's first private-sector trillion-dollar company in 2018; and then the first $2 trillion company just two years later.

Your task in your organization is to be just as clear in your choices. Choose your playground carefully and match it to your strengths.

Isolate that part of the playing field that you can excel in; and then win there by doing things differently from the pack, in ways that add unique value to your chosen customers.

Evolve this positioning as the market changes and as you gain experience.

Boom.

THIRD STEP:
TELL A STORY

*"People don't buy
goods and services.
They buy relations,
stories, and magic."*
—SETH GODIN

Remember Bill Barnett's five-word definition of strategy? "The logic that drives action."

In completing the first two steps of our strategy four-stepper, we have done the logic part—diagnosis and positioning. Good strategy does indeed require good thinking. Dim-witted strategy does not take us anywhere worth going.

But strategy also needs some magic. And for that, we must understand the power of stories.

The Story of Story

Homo Deus was Yuval Noah Harari's sequel to his epic work *Sapiens*. In the later book, Professor Harari asked: Why do humans completely dominate this planet? His answer: Not because we are smarter or more nimble-fingered than the rest, but because we are the only species on earth "capable of cooperating flexibly in large numbers."

That power comes from stories. Most animals, he tells us, have only two realities: the objective reality of the trees, rocks, and rivers outside of them; and the subjective reality of emotional experiences inside them—fear, desire, and joy. Humans have a third reality going on: stories. We construct fictions, and we use these fictions to help us cooperate and make sense of our other two realities. We have moved from the Stone Age to the Silicon Age, says the author, because of the growing power of our web of stories.

Our immense achievements as a species have come from our ability to construct stories around belief systems. We believe there is purpose to our lives; that our leaders should be followed; that nations exist and are worth fighting for; that better days will come if we do certain specific things.

The author posits (based on work done by Nobel laureate Daniel Kahneman) that we have at least two different selves in us: an experiencing self and a narrating self. This is probably the most important explanation of human behavior I have come across in recent years. It elucidates so much.

Harari calls the experiencing self our moment-to-moment consciousness. It is objective and factual. It tells no stories—but it also remembers very little. It is not consulted when big decisions must be made. That authority is given to the narrating self—the storyteller inside us all. The narrating self is not objective. It is biased and partisan, and it tells the story that suits it and makes it feel safe and comfortable.

Pediatricians know this well. After a painful injection, they will give a child a sweet. The final ten seconds of minor pleasure can erase the hours of anxiety and the sharp pain the child experiences. The narrating self censors the worst bits to suit itself. It draws upon the raw data provided by the experiencing self and adds meaning and narrative. And then everything becomes fuzzy and murky.

The point is this: the narrating self is in charge. When you say "I," you are referring to the spiel spun by your storytelling self, not the objective stream of experiences you have undergone. You are referring to the interpretation, not the facts. The mind tries to turn the randomness, cruelties, and frustrations of life into a yarn that stops us from feeling helpless. The yarn may be full of inconsistencies and holes, but so what? The narrator is in charge, not the objective observer. The truth is what "I" say it is. The problem is, we rarely know we are spinning stories rather than telling truths. And sometimes we hold on to the story at all costs, even when our consequent behavior is extremely damaging to those around us.

This is how wars and mass deaths are justified. A story that claims "they did not die in vain" must be told and reinforced by all. That is why we conduct many rituals to "honor" those who perished in mindless carnage caused by a few vested interests. The stories around our tribes, religions, nations, and football teams can cause us to kill or be killed—and be honored for it.

We all choose our stories. Professor Harari tells us that we each have a sophisticated filtering system. We throw most experiences away, but we hang on to a few choice samples and then mix them up with scenes and episodes from our favorite books and movies or words from speeches that impressed us. We craft the story of our identity from these diverse sources.

This identity then drives our actual behavior. If you have convinced yourself that you are a person who is widely respected, you will dismiss all evidence to the contrary and label all your critics haters and losers. If your core story is that of a wise person, you will find it very difficult to own up to your foolishness, even if it occurs regularly. If your narrative is that of the victim, everything in life will seem like a plot against you.

Stories have immense power. That's why your strategy needs a story.

Why? Because of another essential truth: human beings are moved to action only by emotion, not by logic.

Because strategy is mostly a shared pursuit, you need something to *explain* the strategy to your people; and you need to *excite* them with it. Your strategy must become a story.

As Simon Sinek pointed out in his famous TED talk: Martin Luther King Jr. is not famous for his "I have a plan" speech. Had he showed up with charts and diagrams, as most CEOs do, millions would never have been galvanized into action. He revealed his *dream* for America; and those who shared the dream felt the frisson and joined in the mission.

Because strategy is mostly a shared pursuit, you need something to *explain* the strategy to your people; and you need to *excite* them with it. Your strategy must become a story.

Humans love stories. We love listening to them, we love telling them. The earliest remembered connection between parents and children often comes through storytelling; our sense of our own histories is framed by the stories (and myths) we believe about our pasts.

Strategy must become a believable story with a beginning, interesting protagonists, a plotline, and a hoped-for ending. And crucially, those who are to deliver the strategy must feel like characters in the story.

Phil Rosenzweig understood the power of stories in his book *The Halo Effect*. He told us stories are needed to help managers make sense of their world and to help direct their actions. Stories give us the confidence to face the future; they "confer a moral dimension to events."

But Wait: Substance, Not Spin

Before we go any further: your story must not be a farrago of lies.

Rosenzweig's book was actually a scathing critique of the popular delusions and fallacies of modern business practice. He warned against vacuous, feel-good storytelling that acts as a pulpit speech to fire up the brethren—or that reduces business success to a few easily followed steps, available to all.

So please resist the temptation to talk up your strategy, to turn it into a feel-good sermon or a motivational-speaker spiel.

I repeat: a strategy story has only two purposes—to explain and to inspire.

Your story must clarify your strategy and make it understandable. It must create a narrative that others can follow and feel part of. And then it must inspire them to own the strategy and to act on it.

Strategy, remember, is done by humans with humans. And humans love stories. All our books, movies, songs, and paintings are stories.

Story has always been the missing magic in strategy. Most strategies are just banal collections of charts and targets. They inspire no one other than their originator (maybe); they evoke little emotion other than boredom; they are dry and lifeless.

The magic we need, however, is not that of the conjuring trick. We do not need to hide what one hand is doing or use smoke and mirrors to trick our people into believing. We just need to simplify our strategy into a story anyone can understand—and most will want to participate in.

A strategy story that is pure fiction will end in tears when time exposes it to be all make-believe. The skill needed is that of the documentary writer, not the novelist.

Let's Tell a Story

So what does a great strategy story look like?

Think back to what we developed for Apple in earlier chapters—its diagnosis and its positioning. Recall that Apple wished to excel, profitably, in a world of connected devices, by concentrating its efforts at the upper end of the market and by providing standout user experiences.

Can we turn that into a story?

APPLE'S STORY, 2010–20

We give customers a unique world of digital experiences by creating desirable devices and useful services that become central to their lives—and that they happily pay premium prices for.

Only Apple can do this, because only Apple can meld hardware, software, and services seamlessly to create truly special experiences.

I hope you can see that this story is not stretching the truth—it is merely clarifying it in a way their employees can relate to.

It particularly emphasizes key aspects of the strategy: to stand out from the crowd of competitors; to wow customers by making their lives more productive and more fun; and to make premium prices seem fair by giving premium experiences.

It creates a narrative about success, and about Apple's role as the hero of the tale.

What does this story do to the Apple populace?

The Apple designer now knows that good enough ain't good enough—you have to create sighs of pleasure in people using the products.

The Apple coder knows that the software must marry the hardware harmoniously to deliver unique user experiences.

The Apple Store employee knows that customers must be sold technology as though jewelry or fine wines are being purveyed.

The Apple developer knows that being great today is never good enough; Apple must keep several steps ahead of the game and work on tomorrow's products even as today's are being released.

And everyone at Apple knows that the aim is to become a vital part of customers' multifaceted lives.

Does the story work on the average Apple person, though?

Here's a personal anecdote. I often pop into an Apple Store with my family when we're on holiday in any major city.

We once walked into a huge store, spanning two floors of the city's leading mall, located in the highest-rent part of the metropolis. As we strolled in, a blue-shirted employee immediately made eye contact and walked up to us, smiling. We had a complaint, though— one of our iPhones was losing charge unusually rapidly.

The same person looked over the phone, ran a couple of quick tests, and told us this was a known issue. Apple would therefore replace the battery for a nominal charge. It would take only twenty-four hours, and I would be notified as soon as the job was done.

Would we care to look at anything else, she asked? We mentioned a couple of things. She accompanied us throughout, showing us different items on display or on her special handheld device. We found a couple of items to buy, and the same employee checked them out, right where we were—no queueing at a payments counter. Her device did the needful, and a receipt pinged up in my email seconds later.

While chatting with us, she dropped various things into the conversation: for my teenaged son, free learning sessions for youngsters that teach photography skills and video editing; and for me, an SME business service with special benefits.

She was one of dozens of highly engaging, highly diverse employees running around the store. They were all well trained and knowledgeable; looked eager and willing to serve; and between them spoke a wide range of languages. Indeed, the place looked nothing like a store. It was laid out more like a community space where people meet and interact.

These people were delivering the strategy. They were creating huge user gratification; they were justifying their high prices; they were cross-selling other devices and services.

They bought the story.

I left marveling at the thinking. The most expensive location; the best people, deployed in large numbers; quick acceptance of a fault in the product; and a remedy costly to the company offered without needing to fight for it. This, to many businessfolk, is dumb. Why spend so much?

It's not dumb at all; it's extremely sharp thinking. Apple turned its smartphones (and pretty much every product it makes) into luxury items, in a market that traditionally sold just on specs and utility, not brand or reputation. The more than five hundred Apple Stores across twenty-five countries in 2021 are central to this strategy. Apple's products may be great, but there is equal investment in customer experience. The stores provide the high-end, high-touch part of the overall experience. They are used to position the brand, to cross-sell, to create human relationships.

It's not perfect, mind. I have been to Apple Stores that were so overcrowded that no meaningful experience could be had. The consistency of experience certainly does not always extend to retail partners and resellers not owned by Apple. And customers are often forced into buying absurdly high-cost accessories once in the system. But the point is, this company invests in giving its customers unmatched experiences and keeps trying to do it better.

Where does it pay off? In units sold; in selling prices and gross margins competitors can only dream about; in a captive core of well over a billion global customers (and their credit cards) who can be migrated to new products; and, increasingly, to subscription services like music, TV, cloud storage, and payments.

As I write this, Apple hovers around the $2 trillion valuation space. It sits on a cash pile governments can't match. All because it understands customer relationships and customer experiences, and because it invests in lifetime bonding.

Also, because the logical part of its strategy is translated into feelings and narratives that every employee— and indeed most customers—can relate to. The story emerges easily from the strategic thinking, and it inspires action.

Make Your Story Pop

Written down in a couple of sentences, a story can seem anodyne. But it's up to you to bring it to life. Those first words you put down about your strategy story are just the beginning. They are your first attempt to put your strategy across to those who need to understand it.

After that, you should let the story *pop.*

Words are not the only tool at your disposal. Over the years, I have encouraged many organizations to have fun with their strategies and turn them into song, dance, skits, poetry, and even paintings!

Let your strategy leave the boardroom and become a beat on a dance floor, pictures that flow off paintbrushes, words that stream out of the pens of poets, or songs that echo around your corridors.

I have watched many a team unleash great creativity when they are given permission to bring strategy to life, and to depict it in interesting and eye-catching ways.

One of the most unforgettable was one team from a huge corporation that created a mini-play overnight,

featuring the dramatic collapse of their organization—
for *not* doing what was in the strategy. The play culmi-
nated in a TV interview taking place between a well-
known TV personality and *me*—the strategy advisor.
I was played by a senior company director who was
clearly having great fun hamming up my mannerisms
and verbal tics.

"What went wrong with this once majestic organization, Mr. Bindra?" he/I was asked.

"Their strategy never had a story!" he/I answered.

Surreal. This was a meta-story about the power of
story in strategy. I clapped and laughed until I had tears
in my eyes.

Another remarkable depiction: one group I'll never
forget turned the key points of strategic leadership into
a rap song, written and fronted by a well-known chair-
woman and choreographed and performed with great
gusto by a gang of senior executives.

How will you tell *your* strategy story? You must have
a feel for what works in your setting. Release your people from the chains of the usual—graphs on PowerPoint,
dull mechanistic statements, endless spreadsheets. Let
them turn it into images and depictions that resonate.
Remember, your aim is to create an emotional connection to the strategy—so that the people can feel like it
belongs to them, and then act on it.

Let your strategy leave the boardroom and become
a beat on a dance floor, pictures that flow off paint-
brushes, words that stream out of the pens of poets, or
songs that echo around your corridors.

And guess what? Those dancers and singers, those
poets and dramatists you'll need? They're probably

sitting right there in your organization, hidden in plain sight, never previously asked to participate in strategy setting. The bonus achievement is to uncover these hidden talents and allow them to flower—in the service of strategy.

How to Do Story

Let's conclude.

Story is the missing link in strategy. It is the bridge between strategy's logic and the actions that must ensue. It allows people to take charge of strategy and participate in it. It gives employees a *why*, when all they had in the past were hows, whats, wheres, and whens handed down from high up.

Story humanizes the strategy and makes it fit for humans to work with.

The story must not be a fairy tale; it must remain rooted in reality.

The story should be short, simple, and evocative.

The story should take multiple forms. Remove the chains we impose on narrative, and let your people tell the story. Let it enter conversations and echo around watercoolers and chat rooms.

And then, after the story is told and understood, we must act.

FOURTH STEP:
ACT IN CONCERT

"Amateurs talk about strategy. Professionals talk about logistics."
—GENERAL ROBERT BARROW

Your strategy doesn't amount to a hill of beans until *you do something.*

Strategy has always attracted *thinkers* when it actually needs just as many *doers.*

When I was completing university, the two most attractive jobs on offer were in investment banking and strategy consulting. The former attracted those who just wanted to make a truckload of money in their lives and didn't mind becoming glorified hustlers; the latter was for those a little more refined, who had big brains but didn't want to become academics, who wanted to join the smartest people in the world in advising the biggest corporations.

But strategy isn't what you think; it's also what you do. Most strategy consultants are long gone before anything is actually done. A proper strategist, however, hangs around for all four steps in the dance.

The diagnosis, step one in the strategy four-stepper, frames the challenge you face.

The positioning, step two, chooses your battle-grounds and weaponry.

The story, step three, guides and inspires those who must deliver the strategy.

The actions, step four, get the whole show on the road.

A doctor diagnoses what ailment a patient might have by running tests and looking for signals. She then takes a view on the therapeutic approach. The patient is provided with a narrative around the problem and its cure.

But actions must then ensue. Those actions might be surgical interventions, medicines, and dietary changes. Without the final step, the first three amount to nothing. You're just shooting the breeze with the patient.

Richard Rumelt reminded us that strategy is about doing something, not just contemplating it. Concepts must be brought down to earth.

Peter Drucker put the "bringing down to earth" a different way. He told us that if we intend our plans to be more than just good intentions, they must immediately *degenerate into hard work*.

Note the great choice of words, please. If all you're doing is framing *good intentions*, you're not doing strategy. The intentions, noble as they are, must *degenerate*—lose their complexity and become something different. The "something different" here involves the boring stuff—*hard work*. And this transformation of aims into actions must be *immediate*—as the goals are set, so must the actions be.

Rumelt makes a most important point regarding these actions: they must happen in concert—they must be coordinated with one another and work together. The actions involve the setting of priorities and resource allocations that implement the chosen strategy.

Seth Godin put it very well in a blog post a few years back: "All abstract strategy discussions are useless." He continued: "Strategy is worth thinking about if it causes you to make difficult or nonintuitive decisions. And so you have to test your commitment . . . If you can't put an example on the table, a concrete manifestation of the action being discussed, then you're just prattling on, you're not actually serious about strategy."

Strategy, by its very nature, tends to be a little up in the air. We are urged to discuss big issues, look at the big picture, map out overall direction, "helicopter out" of the details—and so we can be forgiven for talking in broad themes and abstractions.

Strategy is about the big things, and yet it is only meaningful if it sweats the details. So where do we draw the line?

The first thing is to recognize the key point: that strategy is meaningless on its own. No matter how deep the intellectual discussion, how innovative the market positioning, or how unique the competitive advantage—it's all pointless unless it leads to something tangible and measurable. Strategy is only useful in terms of the actions it guides you toward. Strategy is only successful if it causes real results on the ground and delivers actual performance improvement.

Otherwise it's pie in the sky, just clever people debating abstractions in pleasant settings.

Here's an example. Many companies today will tell you that one of their strategic goals, or distinctive capabilities, is innovation: the capacity to introduce fresh, game-changing products or solutions. Sounds good, and very necessary in today's fast-moving times. Except that it's usually all concept and no substance.

A single innovative product does not make you an innovator. Having a couple of bright youngsters bubbling with ideas in your organization does not make you innovative.

Innovation as a competitive advantage refers to your continuous capacity to conceptualize, test, and bring to market a series of unique products or services. It's an ongoing thing, not a one-off. So if you are going to label it a key competitive advantage, you have to move quickly from words to facts.

What's your process for coming up with ideas? Who does it? How often? Is it a special event or is it hard-wired into your daily routines? How are ideas tested? How are they developed? How are they filtered? How are they taken to market? What's your target for fresh new products? How do you judge success or failure? What organizational structures support this process? How is innovation rewarded? Which are your next three test products, and when will they reach customers?

That set of questions turns the concept of innovation into an ongoing reality. And those are the questions that most strategy discussions shirk. The actualization of strategy is the proof that it matters and is worth doing.

Choosing the Action Set

To understand what we mean by concerted action sets, let's go back to Apple.

Recall that Apple, from 2010 to 2020, was playing out a certain strategy, focused on achieving distinction in the markets for personal connectivity, entertainment, and productivity. This distinction was to come through intertwining hardware and software in an increasing variety of devices by making that union result in user-friendly experiences, and by building a brand that exuded quality and refinement.

What set of actions would put this show on the road, from 2010 onward? The high-level actions might have looked like the following:

APPLE'S ACTION SETS, 2010–20

Maintain a hyperefficient global supply chain.
Keep refining the devices.
Keep differentiating via software and user experience.
Run a core number of high-end, high-touch stores.
Always be ready to lead the next big thing.

The first action area speaks to the fact that Apple stopped being just American a very long time ago. It had to start keeping its designers in one part of the globe, its manufacturing somewhere else, its stores and customers everywhere. It needed to use the comparative advantage of different locations wherever it was to be found. This global supply chain was set up by Tim Cook—and, tellingly, he became Steve Jobs's chosen successor when the time came. Apple enjoys industry-beating margins not just because it can command high prices for its products, but also because it runs a very efficient global sourcing machine that gets the best prices for premium components. This action set is all about managing collaborations and logistics.

Consumer attention is always focused on devices, though, and here, too, relentless attention and improvements are needed. It is not enough to have a great current iPhone model out in the market—the refinements must keep coming. So Action Two in our list is about paying constant attention to new design features that enhance and upgrade the devices in regular cycles. A one-hit wonder is not strategic—in a fast-changing market, you need a steady stream of winners.

Third, there is the need to keep developing new use cases and ease of use for every device, because that is the key differentiator. Samsung can't do that because it depends on Google and Microsoft for its software. Microsoft couldn't do the hardware part until more recently, when it realized that it also needed some credible physical devices, not just great software. Because this source of differentiation is so key to Apple, Action Three says that a good chunk of the company's people and resources must focus on blending the physical and digital experiences in attractive new ways.

The fourth action set is perhaps the strange one, particularly when it was first introduced. Why should Apple own any retail stores at all? It's a tech company, after all; why invest in the old ways of selling? And not just that, but why look for the most expensive locations in the best parts of town; why make these stores so slick and grand that they look like something out of science-fiction movies? Why populate them with so many expensive shop assistants? The answer is obvious, if you look back to the strategic positioning: top end of the market, aspirational. High-end demands high-touch. That money is worth spending because it strengthens the positioning.

Last, be ready for everything to evaporate and leave you stranded! In consumer tech, whatever advantages you have so carefully cultivated can recede very rapidly. Apple has shown it understands this. It managed to leap from a computer company to a devices one by understanding quite early that what we meant by "computer" was about to change dramatically. It rapidly released a whole slew of products in those years—smartphones, tablets, TV boxes, watches, earphones. The traditional computer became a minority part of the business. That doesn't happen by chance; it happens because there are highly paid, very clever people constantly researching the future of tech in the world and designing prototypes and testing them. The action here is to deploy futurists who barely live in the present. They are the people on the frontlines of new developments, and it is from that the next big thing comes.

Take a look at the five action sets as a whole, and you will notice that they are not detailed. Nor should they be. They simply define the broad areas of coordinated action that must ensue. The devil may well lie in the details, but that devil need not be addressed yet. The granularity must come from others: those whose day job it is to code, to design, to sell, to source—and to dream. Strategists can impose the big actions, but only loosely—the nitty-gritty must come from those on the frontlines.

Note also that we do not just have five independent action sets for Apple. They are connected, and they are coherent. The supply chain provides the best-in-class components that the industrial designers will need in order to create user wows. The always improving devices must be in harmony with software development. The wow in user experiences must rhyme with memorable retail experiences in the stores. And those tasked with living in the future must come back in time, from time to time, to work with those rooted in today's reality.

So what about you? How will you go about isolating your big three, four, five action sets?

The answer lies in the first three steps of the four-stepper. Your action sets must flow out of all the work *already* done in strategy. Your diagnosis, positioning, and story must provide the basis for action—and the *critical action sets must select themselves.* If you are coming up with actions that seem very important but don't chime with the rest of the strategy, something is wrong. Either you missed something earlier on, or you are failing to subtract things from your wish list.

Your three-stepper should throw up the fourth step quite naturally.

If your strategy aspiration is to be the lowest-price provider in your market, then, like Amazon, one of your top actions is to keep relentless pressure on costs.

If unusually excellent customer experiences are key to your strategy, then, like Nordstrom or Taj Hotels, you'd better have an action set that trains and motivates your frontline people to do just that, all the time.

If offering the best content library is your way of winning the streaming wars, then, like Netflix, you might have not one but two action sets focused on this: sourcing the best generic content, and creating your own original shows. Those require different competencies and structures even though they deliver the same win in the market.

If your strategy shouts "digital first," then you can't have digital being done on the fringes of your bank; you have to allow it to come to center stage over time, as Spain's BBVA has done, after starting the journey as early as 2007. This entails enrolling nonbankers in your board and senior teams; it requires investment in multiple external collaborations; and it needs an appetite for running experiments, many of which may fail. Over time, it requires a cultural and structural overhaul.

You'll probably find that the high-level actions suggest themselves and pour out of your team quite quickly. The problem might be to trim them down to what is truly strategic—the *must-do* action sets that deliver the strategy. In the end, I would suggest never having more than six, seven at the outside. Strategy works when it is focused, and having sixteen crucial action areas shows a refusal to focus—or to address things at the correct level of analysis.

Again: do not be tempted to put too much detail in the action sets. You are not designing a straitjacket; you are creating a loose framework that allows others to start contributing the details. Don't overdesign it— allow those who understand the work in depth to come to the strategy part and be useful. The details will come as the work happens. Trust your people to know what it takes to get the right things done.

First, Connect

It's not enough just to define the action sets; they must also be led.

When Angela Ahrendts first arrived at Apple as head of retail, she quickly saw the scale of the task before her. Seventy thousand retail employees, spread across multiple continents and time zones—in a company whose strategy is to provide very consistent, very refined store and online experiences. She admits it took her several months to get going.

Her challenge was to maintain Apple's iconic magic while managing huge crowds in the stores—and the crowds no longer just consisted of the already converted Apple fans. Many "late bloomers" and the merely curious were now thronging the stores.

She needed to show her people that they all mattered, and that they were in service of something bigger than themselves.

That's called leadership.

One quick way Angela found to connect with everyone was to record and disseminate a simple video every Friday: three thoughts in three minutes. She recorded these on the fly, just using her iPhone—no stylized, carefully crafted Apple productions, no studio, no special makeup! Simple heartfelt messages from her mouth to her people on how it's going and what needs to improve. In three minutes.

She described all this to Reid Hoffman during a podcast interview in 2020. Reid is the cofounder of LinkedIn, and his take on Angela's weekly messages was that she understood the need to foster cohesion and shared purpose. "Events, rituals, and good old-fashioned human contact" unite the team.

Get the Kids to School on Time

There's a question I often ask in my seminars, to those in the audience who have young children: "What's your success rate in getting your kids to school on time?"

The answer is almost always in excess of 99 percent.

Getting your kids to school on time, every time, as every parent knows, is no joke. It's a very complicated process. The kids have to wake up early, for one thing—and that's not something you address just in the morning. They have to get to bed on time too, and they have to do that as a habit that's part of the family culture.

Getting your kids to school on time, every time, as every parent knows, is no joke.

The kids have to be dressed and fed before leaving. They have to refrain from distractions. They have to enter the mode of transportation, public or private, on time. Extra time must be built in every day as a buffer, just in case there's an unexpected problem on the way— an accident on the road ahead, a delayed train.

All that is done while parents simultaneously have to get themselves ready for their days.

It shouldn't work, and yet it does—99-plus percent of the time.

Would we not give an arm to get our business strategies executed to that level of success? Why is it that we can't achieve that kind of consistency in organizations?

The answer is that the roots of great execution are not technical—they're *psychological*. You can invest in the best project management tools, but they mean nothing if the people are not invested in success.

Why do kids get to school on time? You know the answer: because they have to. It's not an option. It's not a nice-to-achieve result. It must happen.

First, it must happen because of *hope*. Our children's education is one of the most important things we strive to achieve as humans. Parents make enormous sacrifices and expend relentless energy on getting kids through school. The children's futures depend on it. We hope for them to be better than us, to lead stable and fulfilling lives. And because school education is a key part of that equation, it must happen.

Second, kids get to school because of *fear*. Failure has consequences. There is the everyday fear of getting marked late in the register, and the unwanted possibility of punishments and embarrassments. There is also the greater parental fear of long-term failure—of failed lives and livelihoods. So we don't play games with education.

Note also that if left to the young children themselves, the 99 percent would never happen! Most young kids don't have the conscientiousness and awareness to understand the need acutely. This result is achieved more because the parents make it happen. Wise parents, though, realize early on that a better way of achieving regular success is to build a culture of timeliness in the home and good habits in the children—difficult though that may be.

We rarely take these everyday wisdoms to the office, though. At work, we rely on "carrots and sticks" to get things done. We offer incentives and impose penalties. We offer bribes and inflict diatribes. And so we rarely, if ever, achieve 99 percent execution success.

Lead the Action

Organizations are a minefield when it comes to getting anything of meaning done. Those who have worked in large institutions know that they are a morass of low motivation and trust failure. Most of the people employed there are not going to go the extra mile for anything. They will hold back their discretionary effort and reserve it for other things in their lives. They will get their children to school on time, but they will do the bare minimum to get themselves ahead at work, simply because the conditions for high performance are not present. Most team members do not feel safe or wanted or valued or appreciated; they do not enjoy their daily interactions with their colleagues, and especially their supervisors; and they certainly do not feel any sense of elevated purpose.

This is not their fault. It is a failure of leadership.

Strategy is done by humans with humans, and this is where it usually comes apart.

When you try to get your strategy show moving, understood, and effected by humans, you, too, will face the challenges of low understanding, low commitment, and low engagement.

The ability to simply get important things done is a very underappreciated part of strategy. Having a "let's just do it and see" attitude can lead to dramatic results. Equity Bank Uganda was a tiny, struggling entity not too many years ago. It was quite literally close to the bottom of the heap by most measures. The past few years have seen a dramatic acceleration in deposits, loans, and profitability. Why? Because a rapid execution culture took root, role-modeled by new leadership. Most of what Equity Bank Uganda needed to do in its strategy

---

Strategy is done by humans with humans, and this is where it usually comes apart.

---

was fairly obvious; the challenge was to get all its people ready and willing to do it.

The organization is now right up there with Uganda's leading banks. This trajectory comes from an impatience with too much analysis and an itch to get moving. Things get tried out, quickly, and the organization learns and adjusts as it goes. This "can do" spirit, if it spreads through an organization, can itself be a source of distinction.

In my courses and leadership programs, I emphasize the following four triggers for smart execution of strategy:

1. *Motivate:* People have to *want* to deliver—all over the organization. You don't execute strategy because you have some immaculate charts; you execute it because you've made everyone see the point—and understand their personal contribution to the bigger picture. Motivation comes from a sense of belonging and participation; from appreciation; from being able to make some decisions; and from personal growth during the process.

2. *Communicate*: Angela Ahrendts gets this one. Keep it simple, keep it human, keep it genuine. You have to use the story of your strategy, but you have to bring the story to life, in unique ways. Angela's three-minute videos are a great example of continuous communication that develops the story in real time and lets everyone know what's important, week by week.

3. *Evaluate*: You can't just tell stories and hope for the best, though; you have to measure your progress. Everyone's attention must be focused on the metrics that really matter in a given context—not complicated scorecards, but just the three

or four numbers that reveal how you're really doing. These numbers must flash up frequently, and they must be applauded and addressed as appropriate.

4. *Celebrate*: What do humans love doing? Celebrating! We are wired to commemorate and observe key milestones. Leaders often miss this point entirely. So lost are they in the stress of meeting the deadlines of a crucial project, they forget to pause and celebrate the small wins as they are clocked up. When important milestones are hit—recognize those who have worked all hours to deliver the result. Appreciate them in public and hold little celebrations throughout. Don't wait for big wins; celebrate the small wins too, in small ways. The small wins will lead to the big wins. Good leadership centers on the little things—thanking and appreciating people in a heartfelt way and giving them the heart to carry on.

Make the Strategy Happen

You now know all about turning strategy into actions— the actions that then lead to impacts and results.

Strategy is just a pipe you smoke if you can't have real effects in the real world.

Strategy isn't just what you think; it's what you can get done.

The fourth step in the four-stepper flows from the first three: your strategic action sets are the broad areas of action that will deliver the strategy. They must match up with your view of the challenge, the positioning taken, and the story being told.

Don't define too many action sets—just the most important, highest-level ones.

Many projects, operational plans, budgets, and new initiatives will flow out from these high-level action sets. Those will be done by others and should not be spelled out in detail at the strategic level. Don't make strategy too tight-fitting and restrictive. Leave it loose and comfortable. Leave spaces in your strategy that should be filled by everyone involved in it.

Making things happen is not just about designing the plans; it's a very human endeavor. Execution must be led, wisely and with determination. The best implementations in strategy happen when the people *want* to deliver the strategy, just as much as the bosses do. Success rates and completion rates are high when everyone is invested in the result.

Great execution is more a matter of psychology than anything else. A good strategist ensures a strong psychological contract is in place with those who will execute. The doers are motivated to achieve the strategy.

The best leaders find their own way of communicating strategy continuously, by constantly explaining and refining what matters—in very human language.

The best leaders also lead celebrations. Humans need to grow, and to commemorate their growth. If good stuff is happening on the ground—celebrate.

THE STRATEGY FOUR-STEPPER

"Plans are worthless, but planning is everything."
—PRESIDENT DWIGHT D. EISENHOWER

Now you know the strategy four-stepper in detail. Let's step back and take another look.

What do all four steps look like when viewed together? We have been developing Apple's 2010–2020 four-stepper, piece by piece, as we go. Let's put it all together:

STEP 1: APPLE'S DIAGNOSIS (C. 2010)

Connected devices will rule the world, and the only viable place for Apple to make money is at the top end of the market.

STEP 2: APPLE'S POSITIONING, 2010–20

Where We Play	Where: aspirational, top of the market Where: vertical integration of chips, hardware, software, stores Where: whichever device(s) you prefer Where: services, recurring revenues
How We Win	How: high-touch, high-visibility brand How: the easiest to use How: seamless across devices How: we sell art, not just technology

STEP 3: APPLE'S STORY, 2010–20

We give customers a unique world of digital experiences by creating desirable devices and useful services that become central to their lives—and that they happily pay premium prices for.

Only Apple can do this, because only Apple can meld hardware, software, and services seamlessly to create truly special experiences.

STEP 4: APPLE'S ACTION SETS, 2010–20

Maintain a hyperefficient global supply chain.
Keep refining the devices.
Keep differentiating via software and user experience.
Run a core number of high-end, high-touch stores.
Always be ready to lead the next big thing.

Please take a close look at the complete four-stepper above. I hope you will see the coherence—that it has flow and harmony. We have not just stapled four separate bits of thinking together—the four steps connect.

The diagnosis leads to a positioning, which throws up a story, which turns into top-level actions.

The result: strategy on a page.

That's a summary of strategy that provides the framework to guide the organization at the highest level. It's tight enough to provide guidance, and loose enough to encourage creativity and experimentation.

And that's strategy. It gives you enough nerve to get you on the field of play. Game on!

Apple experienced one of the greatest value additions in business history in the period of 2010 to 2020, so they were clearly onto something. Will the strategy keep evolving? Of course. Apple will learn new lessons from experience; will have missteps as well as unexpected successes; will track new trends; will change its emphasis.

That's how strategy works. It isn't a beautifully thought-out master plan; it's a way of organizing yourself to respond to a big challenge.

Strategy in Your Personal Life

The strategy four-stepper isn't just for corporations, though; it can be applied just as powerfully to individuals and their lives.

Consider yourself a young adult who's just coming of age and pondering the issue of what to do with your life.

The first question, naturally, is: what's really going on in my world, and what do I need to become?

In other words, young-adult you would conduct a quick mental *diagnosis* of the situation, just like a corporation would. What's the real challenge I face? What do I need to become in this life—what does success mean to me?

The next step, quite naturally, involves personal *positioning*. Where should I play, and how will I win? Which careers are open to me? Which ones do I want? Do I want to be employed, or do I want to be my own boss? How badly do I want these options? How do I get the skills and qualifications I will need? How will I stand out from the crowd? How will I get my first foot in the door?

This then leads to a mental *story*: a narrative that both explains the path to be taken and the rationale. It's the personal account of who you are and where you're going—to be told to yourself and to the world. It's your way of carving out a distinctive identity for yourself— something that explains you to others and gives you a narrative arc in your life.

And the last of the four steps? *Act!* Don't just ponder and spin tales—do something. Get that degree or work experience. Learn the skills that you will need. Put yourself out there and make connections. Learn a trade. Spot an unfulfilled need in the world.

Of course, no young adult is going to put down the perfect four-stepper the first time. The more likely result is that a very loose strategy is formulated, perhaps only in the mind, and then the adventure begins. Life decisions often change as life is experienced—and that's not only perfectly OK, it's strategic. When we are faced with uncertainty, a bit of looseness and a willingness to try things out is very sensible.

In sum, the four-stepper is not an artificial construct; it is how we actually all think and act in the face of a challenge, quite naturally. We gauge the situation; we position ourselves to succeed; we create a mental story that explains why we are doing things a particular way; and then we act on the important things that have to be done.

We are all strategists—but not necessarily good ones. Most of us will misunderstand the challenge, follow a misguided path, dream up a far-fetched story, and fail to act with determination.

That's why strategy is *simple*, but it's not *easy*.

Who is the good strategist, then?

The one who can see the signal in the noise and zoom in on the key challenge to be met.

The one who can stand out from the mob of aspirants and do things a little differently, develop some distinction.

The one who uses a simple and powerful story as a motivational and communicational tool.

The one who can see which actions really matter, devote plenty of attention to them, and have the grit to see them through.

You can train yourself to think like a strategist—at each and every stage of your adult life.

Doing the Four-Stepper in Your Head

So far, it might feel like the four-stepper is a formal procedure, something that requires a marker and flip chart or an electronic screen to complete. It can be as formal and rigorous and ponderous as you like—but it can also be quick and instinctive.

Let me take you back to where I began this book. Recall that I was troubled by why I personally did not use formal strategy development approaches in crafting strategy for my own business. Why would I sell something enthusiastically to clients but not use it for myself? If it works for everyone, why not for me?

A good question. Here's the answer.

I used the four-stepper for myself; of course I did. The only difference was that initially I used it instinctively and informally. It was buzzing away in my head all the time—without my being conscious of it or recording any outputs. Without doubt, though: I diagnosed the situation facing me; I took a very particular positioning; I developed a storyline that enthused me, my growing team, and my clients; and I kept acting and acting and acting on the few things that really mattered.

I didn't know it was a four-stepper at the time, and I didn't call it that until much later. But the process of examining my own thinking process made me realize that there was indeed a sequence being followed.

So when should we let the process occur in our heads, and when should we pick up the stylus to bring our four-stepper out into the world?

Good strategists do this thing naturally and instinctively. But unless you are working entirely alone, strategy is something done by humans with other humans. If you are building strategy with a team, you absolutely must not do it alone in your own head!

As my own organization has grown in scale and scope, strategy is being developed by everyone—employees as well as business partners—on an ongoing basis. Not just by the (so-called) strategy guy. Why? Because at the level of the team strategy is a communal act. It emerges from a "hive mind," not a solo brain. I cannot possibly foresee everything that's coming; I cannot process all the variables alone; I do not have the rich knowledge that others do. In fact, as time goes on, I do less and less of the actual thinking, and I act more as a guide.

And: strategy cannot just be handed down to others. It is not a decree that comes down from the mountain; it is developed in the valley where the people are, with the zestful involvement of the people themselves. It must be owned by all, enthusiastically. There are no strategy gods. It's a team sport.

So, then, let your head buzz with the four-stepper—it's a natural way of thinking. But learn also how to turn it into a team activity that is fun, lively, and interactive. Your strategies will become stronger and more robust as a result.

How to See It Coming—Or Not

Let me use an example to show how the four-stepper thinking can become part of your regular foresight.

Suppose you are a restaurant owner—of a single successful eatery, or perhaps a chain of well-patronized outlets. What would your strategy have looked like in 2019?

We all know what happened in 2020 (and continued long into 2021): a dramatic global pandemic shook the world. The coronavirus traveled the globe and jumped into millions of human bodies, causing much illness and social change and economic ruin. Most countries went into a succession of lockdowns and shutdowns and strict social distancing. You did not want to be in the restaurant business in 2020; many millions went out of business, and most suffered dramatic trade slowdowns and had to rethink their businesses.

I ask again: what would your strategy have looked like in 2019—the year *before* the COVID-19 pandemic? Almost no 2019 restaurant strategy would have even mentioned the possibility of a pandemic, let alone planned for one.

I certainly didn't see the coronavirus pandemic coming. I'm a strategy advisor, someone who sifts through the signals the world throws up to discern what might be about to change and what needs a response. But I didn't see this one until it was with us.

In January 2020 many of us were looking forward to a rather different year. Full order books, much travel, many gatherings, a busy office life. By March we were sitting in our homes, looking shell-shocked. Whole economies were shut down, many businesses went into forced hibernation, and millions of workers were laid off.

My first attempt to make sense of the situation centered around the words "black swan." Black swan events were popularized by Nassim Nicholas Taleb. They are unexpected events with a very low probability of occurrence, but with massive impact when they do happen. Sounds like the coronavirus pandemic, no?

No. Mr. Taleb laughs when people call this a black swan. This thing was utterly predictable; it's just that most of us were not paying attention. Similar (but lower-impact) viruses have caused widespread trouble before. Books were written about the big pandemic to come. TED talks were delivered. Hollywood even had movies about it, for crying out loud.

So why were we not paying attention? Anyone following the news in January 2020 should have figured out something big was brewing. Most of us gave only cursory attention to the fact that China had locked down an entire province. Most of us looked away and carried on.

To understand why, we need to know our minds better. Psychologists have identified a particular problem with the way we think. It's called normalcy bias. Most people underestimate the threat posed by looming disasters, be they natural or financial or political, and are plagued by inaction. They underplay both the possibility of the disaster actually happening and the effects it could have on their lives.

This happens even when we have plenty of warning. When governments issue advance alerts of extreme weather events, for example, most people ignore them and try to carry on as normal. Their minds refuse to accept the possibility of severe disruption to their lives; a misplaced optimism kicks in, and they search for multiple justifications for their inaction.

Normalcy bias takes many lives. And ruins many businesses.

Because most of us don't want our lives to change, we convince ourselves that "it's never that serious"—even when it really is. By February 2020 we knew danger was looming. We knew the world was deeply interconnected;

we knew there was more air travel happening than ever before in history; we knew that people would fly while carrying the virus; we knew that it would land inside our borders soon.

We knew, and yet we didn't want to know, because knowing is scary. Knowing means making sharp changes to our lives and livelihoods. We would rather whistle and carry on, hoping for the best.

So there are many reasons why hardly any restaurant chain would have readied itself for a global pandemic. Almost no one is that prescient; almost no one wants to plan for disaster.

However, there is a related trend that should have been obvious to any thoughtful restaurant owner, for many years before 2019—the trend toward in-home dining.

In the years before 2019, more and more women entered the workforce all over the world; traffic jams worsened almost everywhere; a new generation very comfortable with online shopping and very uncomfortable with cooking came onstream; and in-home entertainment options began multiplying.

It should have been easy to see that old-fashioned in-person brick-and-mortar dining would take a major hit regardless. In that sense, the virus just accelerated a trend that was already in play. It did not start a new one.

And so, for many restaurant owners in 2019, an acceptance that home-delivered dining was going to loom large in your life as a mainstream eatery should have featured heavily all over your strategy four-stepper. It should have been part of your diagnosis as a powerful force driving change; it should have been part of your positioning to develop a growing online-ordering service; it should have featured in your story—that you would evolve into offering food experiences away from your traditional physical locations—and developing this more futuristic part of your business should certainly have been in your key strategic actions.

Some restaurant players—mostly in the fast-food segment—were already there. The vast majority simply were not.

By 2021, virtually *everyone* in the restaurant trade was also in the home-dining trade—including some of the fine-dining purists who had sworn it would only ever happen over their dead bodies! Those who had done some thinking, some positioning, some investments, some capacity building in advance—they pivoted very quickly to a world in which in-home dining became a significant part of their business.

Post-corona, restaurant businesses need to be well placed to benefit from two big customer segments: those folks who got used to the convenience of kicking back and getting their favorite dishes delivered to them most of the time, as well as those who want to escape the confines of home and eat in style. Both will coexist. One part of the market is all about speed and ease; the other is about hospitality and ambience. Some will retain the high-touch, full-service dining experience as their core business; others will migrate to cloud kitchens set up for delivery-only service.

Each will have to be the *most* of something. High-touch dining must go big on taste, bonhomie, and atmosphere; delivery food must be algorithmically driven to provide speed and convenience.

That's how good strategy works. You do your best to see the big things coming, but sometimes you miss them completely, and sometimes you see them incompletely. Nonetheless, you keep your business flexible enough to keep repositioning as the world changes. You can't get everything—or even most things—right the first time. The key lesson of strategy is to be ready to learn, unlearn, and relearn as you go, and to try new things out.

Strategy Accelerants and the Classroom

Let's now consider another sector that also got heavily disrupted by the COVID-19 pandemic—education. What did strategic thinking look like for the boards and management teams of schools and universities facing an unprecedented challenge? Picture yourself sitting in those meetings, making decisions at speed.

You had to first quickly think clearly and get to grips with the scale of the problem: was the danger to students, teachers, and parents big enough to warrant total shutdowns? What was more important—safety or continuity?

Would you be able to pivot to remote teaching and learning? Did you have the equipment and infrastructure and staff mindset to pull that off? How much training or investment would be needed? Would you go big on remote—or do the minimum needed in the hope of a quick reopening of schools?

How would you convince your teachers, students, and parents of the wisdom of your decisions? What

You do your best to see the big things coming, but sometimes you miss them completely, and sometimes you see them incompletely. Nonetheless, you keep your business flexible enough to keep repositioning as the world changes.

would your messaging look like at a time of great uncertainty? How would you interact with those who needed to be on board?

What things had to be done rapidly? Health and safety training and new protocols? Procurement and deployment of laptops, routers, and bandwidth for teachers? Constant engagement with government and your fellow institutions? Continuous reassurance to parents and children as schools went into and out of in-person learning?

That's what most schools and universities went

Have the agility to change your dance when the music changes; otherwise, you will be forced off the floor for good.

---

through. I hope you can see by now that the natural flow of thinking outlined above is just the strategy four-stepper: diagnosis, positioning, story, actions.

Some institutions managed to pull off the dance very well; others waffled and fumbled.

What happens post-pandemic, though? Would you treat the whole thing as a bad dream and go back to the good old world of traditional teaching? Many will be tempted to do just that.

That would be a mistake. Traumatic as it was, the novel coronavirus should be seen as a strategy accelerant—it forced us to speed up some of the changes we needed to make in any case. Online education is a case in point. It was bubbling away for years but being resisted by teachers and parents. Suddenly, there was no choice. Education had to be remote, for long periods of time. And by and large, it worked. It might have been messy and glitchy, but people got better at it.

A thoughtful institution would use this moment in human history to rethink the delivery of education. There is no doubt that a good part of education benefits from face-to-face interaction. But all of it? No. The convenience of remote learning throws up many possibilities. Larger classrooms. Lower costs of delivery. Students joining from across geographic borders. Lifelong learning. Why would you throw those opportunities away?

The future is in blended learning—using the best of both worlds. There is so much more to play for when the old boundaries are removed. Thinking like a strategist also involves making the most of a crisis to reimagine the basis for our products and services.

To close this chapter: the coronavirus reminded us of an old and fundamental strategy lesson: have multiple options. Don't be wholly invested in one plan or one platform or one way of doing things. A hyperconnected world throws up many surprises and many disruptions.

Have the agility to change your dance when the music changes; otherwise, you will be forced off the floor for good.

Last and always: stay humble. We feel like the rulers of this planet, but the tiniest of microbes mock us. We feel we have many accomplishments to our names, but we can be undone in moments. To be human is to be gullible, fanciful, and vulnerable. Let us embrace our reality and do good things in spite of it. The strategist does not try to control or predict everything; merely to minimize the surprises and to manage the flow of change.

STRATEGY WISDOMS

"A sailor has to judge the wind, and a ski racer must judge the texture of the snow."
—RICHARD RUMELT

This chapter shares some real-world reflections gleaned from my own strategy journey, as well as some sagacity from strategy's most eminent thinkers.

The Strategy Retreat

I have been less than respectful of the traditional off-site strategy meeting that I discussed earlier in this book. For the most part, this cynicism is warranted. Most such off-sites are just glorified junkets, jamborees disguised as reflection retreats. Real strategy happens in real life in real time, not in special places in special groupings.

Does that mean the strategy off-site is obsolete? Not quite. Strategy retreats can be very useful—if done properly.

It's not a bad thing to take time off from regular work routines and away from regular locales in order to reflect deeply. The spiritual retreat is, after all, a time-honored tradition in life. Time dedicated to deep thought, in a peaceful setting, can be very productive.

What we should not be doing is going on noisy team-building exercises and calling them strategy meetings. Strategy retreats should be just that—a time to talk and reflect, and to do the deep thinking that strategy needs.

The strategy off-site should also not be a time to review business plans and budgets on unending slide decks. That may be a necessary thing to do, but it is a routine office activity that should follow from the strategic thinking—it doesn't displace it, and it shouldn't be conflated with it. A great strategy meeting is a dialogue, a conversation, a cut-and-thrust session. It is a time to reexamine critical assumptions and revisit the competitive landscape. It is a time to design a new future—not a time to derange ourselves with a mind-numbing audit of the past.

Here is some suggested good practice:

- » Use the strategy four-stepper to guide proceedings and give you a structured way of thinking about your strategy. Half a day for each of the four steps is enough to make a good start; a full day for each is ideal if you are taking a week out to tackle this.
- » Use the off-site as a chance to do the strategic stuff that can't usually be done in the office: deep thinking, structured dialogue, peaceful reflection, and consensus building.
- » Invite a speaker or two to guide and provoke you, especially on subjects outside the team's usual expertise. Depending on your industry, topics such as technological disruption, trends in youth culture, geopolitical reconfiguration, and the like might prove to be very instructive. Also, consider a panel of key customers to provide feedback and challenge your team's complacency.
- » Avoid death by PowerPoint! Slideshows have become a mindless management ritual. We do them because we do them. We do them because everyone does them. But if you are there to reevaluate, rethink, and reimagine, then a candid discussion, not

brainless spectatorship, is the key design element for the event. Even the fact that people face a screen rather than each other inhibits discourse.

» Hold Socratic dialogues: small groups of people sit around a circular table and look one another in the eye. The only thing on the table is a single question. They then spend the next hour discussing that question, uncovering hidden complexity, and thrashing out the difficult implications of the question. Both the learning and the outputs are immeasurably better. Examples of great questions:

    » What are we the most of—the best in the market, the most appreciated by customers?

    » How valuable are we to our customers?

    » Which competitors are doing interesting things that we should pay attention to?

    » If you were a competitor, which weakness in us would you focus on to take us down?

    » If we could start this business from scratch, what things would we stop doing immediately?

    » What could make us obsolete?

    » What would give us the right to be here a hundred years from now?

» Attendees at strategy retreats tend to be from the privileged "officer class" of top-tier executives. While expanding numbers would make the event unwieldy, it is a good idea to relax this exclusivity in order to build wider participation in strategy. One way to do this is to invite groups of younger, more-junior employees to some of the sessions. Another is to hold micro-sessions with all employees in structured groups, before or after the senior retreat, that are focused on more-specific challenges and issues.

» Treat the retreat as the beginning of the strategy discussion, not the end. A draft four-stepper is just enough to give you the nerve to do more: test out some assumptions with customers; design specific projects and operating plans; start doing things differently; learn some painful lessons; rethink and reshape.

» Once in a while, hold your off-site in the exact opposite of a quiet, reflective setting! For example, if you are a bank, park the strategy team on the side of your busiest banking hall for a couple of days. If you are a retail chain, congregate at the location with the highest footfall. Why? So that you can look up from your discussions and see actual customers in the process of dealing with your organization. There is no better reality check, and no better antidote to wishful thinking.

> » The post-pandemic world allows us to embrace the virtual interaction as an important element in strategy setting. We no longer need to be confined to the big annual gathering; strategy can be developed and improved as we go now, using digital meetings and real-time updates.

The strategy retreat should be just one of your many ways of developing strategy. Don't make it the centerpiece; otherwise, your strategy process will become both elitist and episodic. Strategy is best when it's a constant stream of consciousness and activity, and when it encourages widespread participation.

Sense and Nonsense

Wherever you craft your strategy—in serene, sylvan settings or in the hubbub of the workplace—it has to make *sense*. Senseless strategy will take you nowhere.

Ah, but which kind of sense do you want your strategy to make?

Jules Goddard and Tony Eccles had the best framing of this question in their book *Uncommon Sense, Common Nonsense.*

Organizations have beliefs about their world. They believe customers value certain things; they believe prices affect demand in certain ways; they believe the market will reward their ways of working. These are just beliefs, until they are tested in the world.

It's necessary to have common sense, but it's not sufficient. It won't win you the big prizes.

Some of these beliefs will pass the test and become *sense*. Others will fail and become *nonsense*.

Markets are battles between belief systems. Competitors put their beliefs to the test. Those who turn out to have more sense than nonsense win the battle. In the authors' words, "strategizing is therefore a discovery process, where the game is won by those who acquire sense and discard nonsense faster than their rivals."

But wait: are all types of sense the same? That was the great insight put forward by Goddard and Eccles: in competitive strategy, it is *uncommon sense* that matters.

Common sense is fine—but it's not distinctive. It's common. Everyone has it; everyone uses it. It becomes table stakes. It's necessary to have common sense, but it's not sufficient. It won't win you the big prizes.

To play big, you need your strategy to zoom in on uncommon sense—the sense that you, and only you, have. Uncommon sense is rare and treasured. It's a truth, but it's your distinctive truth. It is also the basis of great strategy.

Strategy is the quest for uncommon sense.

And that's a great test to put your strategy to, once you have it before you. Is this thing *ours*, preciously so, or is it commonplace? Is it what all our competitors also regard as their strategy? Is there anything at all distinctive about it?

If your strategy can't pass that test, you will run the race, sure, but as an also-ran. You won't win it.

M-PESA now channels a huge chunk of Kenya's GDP—most Kenyans use it to transfer money, make payments, save and borrow instinctively and reflexively. Youngsters take it for granted. But never forget—when Safaricom's M-PESA was first birthed, it made no sense at all! In 2007, sending money by SMS was a crazy idea—uncommon nonsense. Banks laughed it off—they saw no threat to their business at all. And yet, when the belief was brought to the market for testing, the numbers went through the roof dramatically. Nonsense became sense, and the sense, because it was uncommon, was exclusive to Safaricom. They now held all the cards.

Netflix's early idea about streaming entertainment into homes was uncommon nonsense—until it became uncommon sense.

Coca-Cola's idea about selling a sugary drink as a lifestyle ingredient, a vibe, a buzz was uncommon nonsense—until it became uncommon sense.

Instagram's idea about becoming the world's photo album, with its users' every meal, trip, and mood on open display, was uncommon nonsense—until it became uncommon sense.

AirBnB's idea about renting homes out for short stays at scale using a mobile app was uncommon nonsense—until it became uncommon sense.

Kenya's tiny Equity Building Society once had the idea of becoming the bank of the poor and underserved, and it dreamed of becoming a pan-African giant. All uncommon nonsense at the time—now uncommon sense.

Are any of your ideas uncommon sense in the making? You will only know by building your strategy on the uncommon rather than the common, and then taking it to the world to be tested and for the truth to be revealed.

Really Hard

Scott Galloway has an equally interesting take. Strategy, he tells us, is the answer to the question, "What can we do that is really hard?"

Take a closer look at the world's really successful organizations. What they do, folks, is really hard. If we could all do it, it would be easy. But we can't.

Amazon has a vicelike grip on e-commerce, order fulfilment, and web back ends, among many other things. That stuff is really hard. Try it and see.

Coca-Cola owns distribution. Its products are everywhere. See if you can pull that off.

Elite hotel groups like Taj, Oberoi, Mandarin Oriental, or Four Seasons deliver consistently excellent guest experiences across properties, no matter which set of employees is involved. Do you want to give that a go?

Excellence is earned. It takes years of toil and trouble. It has many stop-starts and sleepless nights. It requires dedication and endurance. Are you up for that? Elite military units build cultures and skills by repeatedly training and retraining their people. Top soccer teams instill a style of play that takes years to come to fruition. Rescue organizations drum in a sense of overriding purpose, supported by endless drills and rehearsals that turn their people into heroes when disaster strikes.

If your strategy is focused on doing just the easy stuff, it isn't strategy. If it feels undemanding, a doddle, or a cinch, then you're on the wrong track. Your strategy should make you break out in a sweat just contemplating it. Doing hard things will give you the breakthroughs and the distinctions. The easy path is the road to mediocrity.

Slapstick Strategy

When I was a boy, Groucho Marx really made me laugh. That moustache, the cigar, the crazy walk, the biting wit—I lapped it up. But where did his stage and screen persona come from?

Groucho's world-beating comic performances have enthralled many generations of viewers. They seem smooth, spontaneous, and effortless—a natural comic genius, you might think. Groucho was indeed a genius, but not because he was born with it; he was a genius because he was willing to keep trying different things and improving his act bit by painful bit. He once wrote about the comical character he crafted:

> It was developed by groping,
> trying out, grabbing at any
> material that offered itself. I was
> just kidding around one day,
> and started to walk funny. The
> audience liked it, so I kept it in.
> I would try a line and leave it in
> too if it got a laugh. If it didn't,
> I'd take it out and put in another.
> Pretty soon I had a character.

That reveal is contained in the book *Making Innovation Work*, by Tony Davila, Marc Epstein, and Robert Shelton. The Marx Brothers became one of the world's most renowned comedy acts. Not because they had innate, natural talent—but because they tried stuff out and learned what worked and what didn't.

I was delighted to read what Groucho Marx had to say about their famous act. What is he saying? That it's not about innate creative talent or effortless idea generation at all; innovation is all about hard graft and a willingness to try things out.

As the book explains, Groucho also knew how to commercialize his ideas by trying things out in the creative marketplace—stage shows, clubs, radio—and then taking them to the film world when the first motion pictures took off. In business, innovation is futile if it can't be brought to market at a profit.

After much trying, fumbling, improvising—"Pretty soon I had a character." If you substitute the word "character" with "strategy," you will see why I'm so keen on this story. In my experience, the best strategies are also formed in this way. They do not come from blinding flashes of brilliance, or epiphanies encountered during strategy retreats on lakeshores. They come from acute observation of what the market likes, and from a systematic and disciplined process of trial and error.

So try stuff out, people. Don't pretend that you can get it all right the first time, or that you have a beautifully refined strategy that you can showcase to the world. That strategy document sitting on your shelf, which you show so proudly to visitors, is a piece of fiction. You can't plan out the world ahead—you can only prepare for it and take advantage of it.

Innovative strategies are the result of many burned fingers, failed projects, and trashed ideas. Life's like that. It's painful and annoying. But those who persist emerge victorious. Most importantly, ideas need to be tested in the marketplace. That's what Groucho Marx was doing: trying ideas out on his customers, and then refining and polishing them until he had something sublime. His nonsense became unique business sense; his hard grind paid off.

Strategy is not developed in great cloudbursts of creative thought. Most of the time it is developed through the far more mundane process of trying and failing. I hate to disappoint all of you creative geniuses out there; but in my experience, a great strategy just emerges, slowly and often painfully. People make a bet on something; they try to do it; they get it wrong; then they learn to do it better, and better, and better. Eventually, they become so good at it that the world stops and takes notice (and people like me start writing about it).

Strategy is not developed in great cloudbursts of creative thought. Most of the time it is developed through the far more mundane process of trying and failing.

Plain Dumb Luck

We've discussed many successful organizations and individuals in this book. We've outlined the strategies they used to guide and drive their success. We've provided a simple four-step process that you, too, can use to frame your strategy.

But in addition to insights and frameworks, guess what else you'll need?

Shake Shack is a very successful restaurant chain, valued today at more than $3 billion. But it had very humble origins—a single hot-dog cart. So how did this happen?

Danny Meyer was deeply interested in restaurants from a young age, and he turned down law school to enter a low-prestige, high-risk industry—against most people's advice and against his father's wishes. And he entered not from a position of theory and intellect, but by actually working at restaurants in junior positions—understanding the cooking and serving of good food.

In the mid-1980s, Danny Meyer opened his first outlet, in Manhattan. What did he do first before opening? He walked around. He walked and walked, and he observed the neighborhood, the people, the facilities. He was doing the "sound of the river" exercise that I introduced in chapter 4. Eventually he found a spot he regarded as perfect, but there was already a restaurant there. He approached the owner and bought it out, taking on a fourteen-year lease with no prior restaurant-owning experience. The money was raised by borrowing from relatives.

That was the Union Square Cafe. His idea was this: high-end food, but served in a casual, welcoming environment. The cuisine and style were a hit, and patronage increased quickly. Meyer became confident enough to open a second restaurant, with its own name and individual identity—but please note that it was a full nine years later. The Union Square Hospitality Group now runs a stable of individual restaurants.

How did this fine-dining group venture into milk-shakes and fast food, though?

A single hot-dog cart was opened in Madison Square. This was a temporary nonprofit venture, part of a collective community initiative to rehabilitate the area. The food became so popular that a permanent kiosk was created, serving the now-famous dogs, but adding burgers and shakes. Shake Shack was born.

The founder's idea was not just food—but hospitality as well. Hospitality is different from service, Meyer tells us. Service is what you do; hospitality is a warm feeling you create in the recipient. Combining ordinary food with hospitality is what led to a whole new category of restaurant: fast food made well and served with heart.

There was no intention to create a chain, however; the second Shack did not open until many years later—and that, too, was only done to relieve the long queues at the first one. Number two also generated huge queues, though, and so the idea took root and Shake Shack eventually became a separate business, dwarfing its origins. Today there are more than 275 outlets across fourteen countries.

To what does the founder attribute this success? What was so different? It's the hospitality, says Meyer. Food you know, which evokes childhood memories; done better than you expected; served by people who are nice to you. Ka-ching.

One must never extrapolate just from one person's success, or learn universal lessons from one experience, but there are nonetheless some timeless truths about strategy and enterprise in there. Did you spot them?

First, before you even begin: are you committed to this industry, this product, this set of customers? Do you want this to happen; will you go all in? Or is it just one option in your portfolio of possibilities? Commitment makes all the difference.

Next, don't begin with a spreadsheet; start with the product and the customer. Understand how things are made, why they are needed, and how they're consumed. Roll up your sleeves and do the nitty-gritty in your early years. Take it slowly; don't rush to expand and ruin what makes you special. Be ready to fail too—but learn and keep going.

Danny Meyer shared the best advice about business, which he got from his grandfather: stop complaining about problems; problems are the definition of business. The best entrepreneurs are not those with fewer problems; they are the ones who solve them better. Meyer took this thought further—with whom do you want to solve those problems? Who should be alongside you? He built a team of like-minded comrades based on emotional skills, not just technical ones.

So: learn the basics by doing them, not just studying them; learn through interaction and experience; grow slowly but surely; and as you grow, build a team of folks that you actually enjoy being around.

I listened to Danny Meyer talking about Shake Shack and success with Guy Raz on NPR in June 2020. When asked about what drove his personal success, he went quickly to good luck—in fact, he attributed 80 percent of his achievements to luck, and just 20 percent to a work ethic.

Why would that be, though? The man put in the hard work—he cooked food and served it when he founded his first restaurants. He walked the streets incessantly to understand the lay of the land before opening any outlet. He demonstrated important personal traits when expanding, such as patience and a willingness to grow slowly. He had a powerful insight—that success in the restaurant industry is as much about hospitality and experiences as it is about the quality of the food.

This is a man who understood the strategy four-stepper without ever learning it. He observed the local market keenly, and he generated his insights by walking around and learning the trade. He took positionings based on gaps in the market and on what he felt able to deliver, and he saw that good old-fashioned hospitality was the missing link. He created a strong narrative around his ideas. And he acted decisively by delivering the ideas through a like-minded team.

Doesn't all of that matter? Of course it does—but only when coupled tightly with a strong dose of luck.

How did this luck feature in Meyer's life? First, he won in the genetic lottery. He was born to relatively affluent white parents in a country that celebrated and supported entrepreneurship. He was able to raise his initial seed capital from his own relatives—enough to open a high-end restaurant in a high-end area. Such advantages do not flow to all.

Timing was also on his side. He made some of his key moves during buoyant times in the economy. And as he himself readily points out, serendipitous connections early in his life led to favorable reviews of his first restaurants, and chance events led to huge crowds appearing at key points in the early trajectory of his fast-food venture.

Luck alone is not enough, do note: Meyer was able to take advantage of the good fortune when it popped up. He made and served good food, after all—but so do many others. Luck provided the wind in the sails at key moments.

Danny Meyer also has the wisdom to know something else: success is never just about you, no matter how unique your qualities. Other people pay a huge role. The world likes to highlight individuals, but it is mostly teams that clock the real achievements. I have been paying attention to high achievers and great leaders for much of my life, and I notice this every time: whether or not the world sees it, there's always a good team driving exceptional performance.

Most successful entrepreneurs are often lost up their own backsides, imagining that their achievements flow from endogenous factors in their lives—forces of their own making. Actually, much success is explained by stochastic exogeneity—random things that are nothing to do with us.

The real lesson is to be found in the definition of luck attributed to Seneca: luck is what happens when *preparation meets opportunity*. The wise don't downplay the role of random good fortune; they prepare to take advantage of it. They do all the good things they have to, knowing full well that fortuity is also needed. So that when opportunity arrives, it meets a well-prepared strategist ready for many possibilities.

We must inculcate good personal traits and practices; we must come up with novel approaches, but we must also understand that the dice will fall in unpredictable ways throughout our lives. Sometimes fortune will knock us back, and sometimes it will work in our favor. The trick is to be ready regardless.

The special seasoning as you cook your own four-stepper? Sheer, simple luck. You'll need it.

Meet Your Strategy Consultant

I was a very active strategy consultant in Europe and Africa for the better part of two decades. I have a lifetime treasury of consulting involvements behind me: blue-chip banks and insurance companies, disaster-relief agencies, anti-corruption authorities, telcos, brewers, media houses, and many more.

Make no mistake: good consultants are vital to most large organizations. A good consultant has developed deep knowledge and expertise of the kind that a busy executive will never be able to. A good consultant has also experienced a wide range of contexts that a line manager will struggle to clock. A good consultant has both depth and scope and can therefore be eminently useful.

Note my repeated use of "good," though. Many consultants are anything but good: their expertise is often shallow and superficial, and their experiences are limited and short-lived. From big-name firms to solo practitioners, the profession has a lot to answer for and much hokum and chicanery that it has inflicted on the world over the years. Indeed, many of the global headline failures of recent times have had highly paid consultants involved all the way to disaster.

This is because there are many potential fault lines in the relationship between client and consultant. First, people who most actively and avidly seek external consultants are often those who do very little to develop in-house expertise and who want the quick-and-dirty solution of hired help. Second, consultants are often brought in to do the CEO's dirty work—hired guns who give the appearance of independent validation and provide a convenient curtain for the CEO to hide behind. Third, consultants can become a never-ending drug that ultimately weakens the organization.

Do external consultants have any role to play in your strategy?

Yes, they do, in a limited, special way.

Do not outsource your strategy-making—lock, stock, and barrel—to consultants, no matter how reputable or qualified they are. Strategy is, at its heart, your personal endeavor. It should come out of you, and it should reflect you, your values, and your standards. The best strategy is peculiar and idiosyncratic.

An outsider cannot do that for you. Outsiders are not invested in your uniqueness; they are invested in making you like their other clients so that their knowledge can be spread across their portfolio.

Much large-scale consulting turns into a production line. The same research and insights are applied to all clients; very similar positionings and actions are recommended to all. There is very little that is bespoke about the process. You will probably end up with an ill-fitting off-the-rack suit that has little to do with the specific contours of your organization.

A strategy that comes from outside the body can be like a transplanted organ. Your people will reject

---

Your best strategy consultant is *you.* Get help and support for your strategy by all means, but don't abdicate the role.

---

it. They'll smile and play ball, sure—but good luck with getting anything implemented. The best strategies are developed internally, with the explicit backing and involvement of the chief executive; with the hearty involvement of as many employees as possible; and within the quirks and eccentricities of the internal culture.

Also, bear in mind one of the core messages of this book: strategy is not a one-off event. It is an evolving process of ideation, experimentation, and edification.

Which outsider will manage that for you, and for how long and at what cost?

Here, though, is what you *can* use external consultants for in strategy:

» To provoke thinking and enrich the discourse with specific expertise that's not available in-house, and to share industry research and insights.

» To inject vigor and fresh thinking drawn from a range of other industries into your own deliberations and discussions.

» To raise the game for your own people by exposing them to leading-edge thinking.

» To run specific parts of the strategy journey, such as research projects, data generation and analysis, or pilot projects that test the path ahead.

» To challenge your team to play bigger and to provide an independent sounding board for your ideas.

The best consultant is your journey guide, not your paid companion or hired hand. The onus is on you to develop your own people and capacity to do strategy properly, in your own way. If you are unable to do strategy without outside help, something is very wrong with your organization. The flaws run deep, and perhaps those should be addressed first.

Like every market, this one has its share of bad buyers, bad sellers, and bad practices. Discerning selection and limited deployment should be the watchwords.

Your best strategy consultant is *you*. Get help and support for your strategy by all means, but don't abdicate the role. A truly great consultant would be the one who helps you do it all by yourself and walks away, fulfilled, when you do.

It's the Culture, Stupid

The heading of this section is the answer to the question: Guess what's even more important than strategy?

When the astronomers of yore were peering into the night sky and trying to make sense of the different twinkling shapes they saw up there, they were limited by one major constraint: their own eyes. Until telescopes were invented, we could not even tell the major differences between the celestial bodies.

When the first telescopes appeared, we were able to discern between stars, planets, and moons—but only those that were closest to us. For a long time, mankind thought there were only two or three planets with properties similar to ours in our solar system. Mercury, Venus, and Mars were known by Babylonian and Mayan astronomers in antiquity. Jupiter and Saturn were visible to those looking for them, but only as notable far-off objects. Only Galileo worked out, centuries later and using a rudimentary telescope, that the earth moves around the sun—for which revelation he was imprisoned. It was not until the twentieth century that we could map out our solar system with any certitude.

Long before advanced telescopes revealed the truth, however, the suspicion remained that other large bodies must exist in our locality. Those mathematically inclined could discern that there was a gravitational tug acting on the bodies we could see and track. Their orbits suggested hidden planets that could be pulling at our earth and its neighbors.

When telescope technology advanced to allow us to see far enough, there they were: all the planets in our solar system that had been silently distorting our path for eons. Yet even today, there is uncertainty about an undiscovered "planet nine."

In management, we are right now in the position of those early astronomers. We study what is visible, but we suspect there is some giant hidden force exerting a pull on our activities and shaping our direction. We can't see what it is, but it is there.

That force, that hidden giant planet, is *culture*.

We can see strategy, see operations, see people and performance, see technology. We act on all those things and shape their paths. But we know something big distorts the path of all those "planets." The hidden giant: culture.

I can't recall where I first came across this metaphor—of culture being the hidden planet—so I sadly can't attribute it, but I know a light bulb went off in my head at the time. All those strategies we work on so meticulously, not knowing that their path will be distorted by the big unseen force . . .

Once you see culture, you can't unsee it.

With your new advanced telescope, you see the tug that culture has on strategy. You might devise a breakthrough strategy that is ambitious and far-reaching and game-changing. Yet you will probably never execute it, simply because a greater force will take over.

Strategy is what you think you'll do; culture is what you'll actually do.

People behave in preset ways, delineated by their culture. The simplest definition of culture is something like this: *the way people think, respond, and behave in a group.* But wait, why *do* most people behave just like the group does, most of the time? Because the human being is a social creature who has evolved through observation and mimicry and cooperation. Because we gain status from being prominent members of our groups and lose status (at least initially) from being outliers.

So culture exerts a really, really powerful pull on most members of the group.

If your strategy requires your people to behave in fresh new ways, red alert! Just having a great new strategy, no matter how logically or emotionally compelling, will not change culture. Culture responds to a wholly different range of influences.

In fact, some of the most telling modern insights about culture suggest you can't *choose* to change it at all! Contrarian consultant Niels Pflaeging (in his book *Organize for Complexity*) compares culture to a shadow. You can't change a shadow, but it changes all the time!

This rings so true. You don't change culture by working on it directly. You work on the things that culture is a shadow of. You work on the code behind the interface. "Culture is not a success factor," he says, "but an effect of success or failure."

What then, are the things that drive culture? What's causing the shadow? Who's writing the code? My thoughts, based on years of observation:

» *Leadership*, at all levels, affects culture. Leaders influence culture more than anyone else. The example they set matters more than anything else. Their behaviors set the tone for everyone else. The workforce's sense of what is important and what is rewarded comes from observation of leaders.

» *Boundaries* tell everyone what the limits of behavior are. What is rewarded and applauded? What is penalized and punished? Showing people clear boundaries—do this and we will appreciate you, do that and we will spurn you—provides clear cultural signals to the organization. Shock tactics—disproportionate rewards or penalties—can move culture (relatively) quickly.

» *Success* shapes culture by reinforcing the behaviors that drive that success. If your strategy succeeds and your organization goes places, it will naturally repeat and support all the ways of working, all the practices that have caused the success to happen.

When I first visited Singapore, I was struck by how clean the city-state was. Yet a short car ride away are its messy neighbors. Why such a stark difference?

For one thing, no one litters. Try it and see, said one taxi driver to me. You will be caught on camera, and the fine will make your eyes water. If you persist in doing it, you will be made to clean the roads with your fellow litterers. And if that doesn't cure you, you will be jailed. For littering.

Clearly, someone *really* wanted a clean city!

The shock tactics accelerate the behavior being demanded. But wait—it was a generation ago that these rules came into place and were vigorously enforced. Today, hardly anyone is tempted to litter, or punished. Singapore's people regard cleanliness as their innate culture. A new generation was born knowing no other way.

Do note, however, that had the strategy of orderliness and cleanliness and respect for rules *not* been associated with economic success, perhaps the culture would have reverted to living with the disorder of old.

Culture is a whole book in itself, but let's end with some pointers on the relationship between culture and strategy.

Culture is stronger than strategy, but strategy can reshape culture—*but only if strategy succeeds*, and *only over time*.

If your existing culture is very strong and not supportive of your new strategy, you will have mountains to climb as you struggle to reshape behavior.

Culture is one of the great enablers of strategy, and also one of its great impediments. Wise leaders recognize this conundrum, and they work on culture and strategy concurrently, never letting one get out of sync with the other.

The best way to work on culture is to work on leadership, on role modeling the desired behaviors, and on the clear communication and enforcement of boundaries. And still, the effects will take a long time to come through. People don't change their behavior just because you ask them to; they change it because the conditions that they respond to change. And they do it slowly.

If you lead people well, and you lead them into good strategies, your culture will be just fine. If you don't, it will be your biggest problem.

Strategy Is Also the Next Five Minutes

I'm a big fan of Tom Peters. He is one of the few gurus out there who brings strategy down to the ground, where it belongs. He makes it real and actionable, not all theory and no thump.

In his last two books, Tom trumpets that excellence is not a long-term aspiration. Excellence is the next five minutes.

By which he means: What are you just about to do? Are you committed to making that thing the best it can possibly be? The next five minutes could be the conversation you are just about to have with a team member—will it create an impetus to do something to a high standard? Will it energize that person to aim higher? The next five minutes could be a phone call you are about to make to a customer. Will you be listening carefully and noting what you need to do to improve your product, or will you be shaking your head and making excuses? The next five minutes could be the email you are about to write. Will you think it through properly, make sure you don't make silly grammatical errors, be clear, and be precise?

Excellence, in other words, will not come from that long-term cultural change project you are initiating in order to make your organization more agile and more innovative; it will not come from the product quality enhancement initiative you have commissioned on the factory floor; it will not come from the new enterprise-wide IT system you are planning so that you can serve customers better.

Excellence comes from the leader, first and foremost. And five minutes of observing a leader in action can reveal whether this leader has it in them to set the standard for the brutally demanding things that genuine excellence entails. A leader who doesn't listen, who doesn't empathize, who doesn't bother with niceties, who doesn't care about outcomes—that leader ain't creating excellence anytime soon. No matter how much is about to be spent on strategies and projects and transformations.

Excellence also comes from you. From not waiting for your leaders to become excellent, or for your facilities to be modernized. Excellence is also *your* next five minutes. How well will you do the task you are working on right now? How engaged will you be in solving a problem in the meeting you're sitting in? How helpful will you be with the colleague who's facing a deadline?

Because if we can't be excellent in the moment, this moment, we can't be excellent in the future. True achievement does not depend on having all your ducks in a row, all systems in place, all support mechanisms working. It comes from doing the best you can with what you have at the time you have it. It is a mindset, not an aspiration.

No matter how good your strategy, how painstakingly developed, how superior to all the pretenders out there—it evaporates one day.

When you are committed to giving everything your best shot, your shots will only get better. When you work your socks off to do well, the paths to success will reveal themselves. Good strategies will emerge; worthwhile projects will be undertaken; results will ensue. Great leaders spend every minute being the best they can be for others. Without the excellence mindset, however, most things will fall on rocky ground.

Strategy need not be a grand exercise in contemplation and analysis, starting in the clouds and trickling down. It can also be built from the ground up—one good action at a time. When we do individual tasks well, those tasks have good payoffs. The payoffs lead to repetitions, and the repetitions lead to patterns. *The patterns become our strategy.*

Now stop and think about what your next five minutes look like.

And Then It Evaporates

So you've done all the hard work of strategy.

You spotted the key trends in your market, and you prepared yourself to meet the coming challenge of your time and industry.

You took a positioning that allowed you to deliver superior value to a group of customers.

You crafted a narrative about your strategy that rang true and inspired the troops—and they enrolled in the mission.

You isolated a few top action sets and got everyone working on them.

You made sure your organizational culture was in harmony with your strategy because you have always paid attention to culture and allowed it to evolve.

You did all that, and then everything evaporated!

That, sadly, is the fate that awaits you—and every strategy.

That's the killer punch: it doesn't last. No matter how good your strategy, how painstakingly developed, how superior to all the pretenders out there—it evaporates one day. All that work will disappear into the ether. All that will remain is what you have learned, and what you can apply in starting all over again.

Your competitors will eventually learn your tricks and replicate them—or discover new tricks you hadn't seen coming.

Your customers will eventually tire of your proposition, start finding it meh, and want to move on.

Technology will disrupt your industry just when you were feeling comfortable and settled, and it will rewrite the rules of engagement.

Regulators will view your success with suspicion and heap a new array of antitrust measures and rules on you.

Some or possibly all of those things are going to happen to you, no matter how successful you feel at present—or perhaps because of it.

Up until around 2005, Microsoft had a complete stranglehold on the world of computing. It seemed utterly impregnable. And then it teetered because it missed some of the biggest trends in the industry. It has bounced back now, but only after a comprehensive strategy reboot.

Sears, Debenhams, Borders, Toys "R" Us, and many others were retail's icons, giants who could not be felled. Until they were, by the onslaught of online shopping and by their own errors of judgment.

GE was the world's most valuable corporation in 2005. It was applauded for its strategy and its leadership.

Books were written about it, as an example to others. Its finance division, GE Capital, was bigger than most banks. Today it is no longer in the top one hundred most valued companies, and market sentiment sees the conglomerate as being sold for body parts in order to stay alive.

In 2007 BlackBerry owned the high-end smartphones market. Every corporate honcho sported one. It conveyed both utility and status to its users. Its parent firm, RIM, had a great strategy. But 2007 was also the year the iPhone arrived. BlackBerry's leaders mocked it, failing to note the upheaval in personal computing that was heralded. Apple and Google, however, had seen it very clearly and acted on it. By 2012 RIM's joint CEOs were gone. By the end of 2014, RIM's market share had collapsed to 1 percent.

Things change. People change. Circumstances change. Times change. *You* change.

If your strategy doesn't change as well, you will be left talking about the good old days while others take charge of the even better new days.

All the great companies and organizations and products discussed in this book will also fade away after their time is done—unless they renew themselves afresh. No matter how good your strategies are today, they can't help you when the game changes.

Today's technology giants can seem indomitable, but all human empires come unstuck eventually. Network effects are creating unprecedented personal fortunes and power for the individuals heading these organizations, and that unhealthy concentration is likely to itself be the harbinger of change. Overinflated egos cause many a crash.

This is the final trait of the great strategist: never to take your success for granted; never to get high on your own supply; never to assume what is great today will remain great tomorrow.

If you have a great strategy behind you, look around. Do you see energy and enthusiasm in every board and management meeting, or just superficial box-ticking? Do you get lively repartee and intelligent probing going on, or just dazed expressions?

Do you see self-satisfied directors and managers, enjoying yesterday's successes without developing tomorrow's positioning? Very little time spent on strategy, innovation, and futuristic thinking? Big perks and retainers that inhibit any rocking of the boat? Do you see decision-making that's heavy on formality but light on substance? Is "If it ain't broke, don't fix it" one of your organization's favorite phrases?

Then I'm afraid trouble is brewing. It's not enough to have a great past in business; the future is never assured, and it must be built afresh.

Yes, some things are timeless and don't need constant tinkering. But that can't be the abiding slogan of the strategist. The strategist says, "If it ain't broke, let's build the next thing before this one breaks."

If you're a forward-thinking leader, you need to be very aware of this tendency to stick to what's easy, what's been done before, what involves few risks. It's a natural human proclivity to stick with that which is comfortable and known to work. But it's very, very dangerous in certain circumstances.

Life throws some unpalatable realities at us. Nothing really lasts. Most things have a season, and then they are gone. Our successes are only partly our own doing. Change occurs and undoes our pasts. Randomness features heavily in our lives, for better or for worse. Meaning is elusive.

If we can develop the fortitude to cope with these realities, we have a better chance of coping with our twisting lives. If we can see through our own myths and smoke screens, we might be able to handle change and entropy differently.

Stay hungry, stay curious, stay suspended in a state of wonder. Great strategy is not a one-off; it is a continuing game of twists and turns. The point at which you feel most accomplished and most fulfilled as a strategist is the point at which you should become the most alert. As Sam Cooke sang, "A Change Is Gonna Come."

It always does.

WHAT IS STRATEGY FOR?

"He who has a why to live for can bear almost any how."
—FRIEDRICH NIETZSCHE

Does this happen to you? Every so often, in the throes of activity, you get pulled up short by the question: "What is all this *for*?"

What do we strive for? Why are we always so busy? What are we aiming for? What is success?

The point of this book was to turn you into a strategist—someone who can connect people in shared responses to the core challenges of your life.

What will you do with that power, though?

Will you just design and deliver strategies that outdo your competitors? That make your annual profit targets? That meet with board approval? That make your shareholders a little richer? That generate applause for you?

The ultimate goal of the great strategist is something far better than those mundane aims. It is to use strategy to play a longer, more important game.

What's Your Game?

A question for you: do you remember something called the "Zune"?

Not really, I guess.

Another question: do you remember something called the "iPod"?

Of course you do.

Both were MP3 music players. Here's the thing, though. The Zune, made by Microsoft, was the far superior product in most respects. And yet it failed miserably and was discontinued a couple of years after its launch. The iPod, made by Apple, was the dominant device of its time.

The story is told to very good effect by Simon Sinek in his book *The Infinite Game*. Mr. Sinek spoke some years back at a Microsoft event, and then at an Apple event a few months later. The Microsoft of the time, under the leadership of Steve Ballmer, was obsessed with beating the resurgent Apple. The Zune was part of that strategy, to take on the iPod that was then so popular with the youth of the world.

The product was great, reports Mr. Sinek. He was given a Zune as a gift after the event, and he found it elegantly designed with a simple and intuitive user interface. And yet he gave it away—mainly because he could not connect it to iTunes, which housed most of his music collection.

After the Apple event a few months later (in which Microsoft was never mentioned), Mr. Sinek was sharing a taxi with a very senior Apple executive. He couldn't resist telling this gentleman: "You know . . . I spoke at Microsoft, and they gave me their new Zune, and I have to tell you, it is so much better than your iPod Touch."

The reply he got was a smile and a single sentence: "I have no doubt."

Mr. Sinek's reflections on that response led eventually to his excellent book. In it, he surmises that Apple plays an *infinite game* in business—a game without end. Mr. Ballmer's Microsoft was playing a *finite game*—one that tries to win by achieving arbitrary metrics over an arbitrary time frame.

Finite game players try to win in the short term. Infinite game players try to stay in the game—even after they personally have left the field. The former are fixated on quarterly targets, market share, and personal bonuses. The latter have a bigger deal going on. Their aim is to stay relevant and useful in perpetuity, not to suck value out of the market for personal, short-lived glory.

Apple was not concerned that a competitor had a "better" product. It recognized that the infinite game produces many ups and downs, many wins and losses. Its aim was to help people listen to their music and carry it around.

To that end, the iPod also lost out. After a sterling run, it faded away—killed by Apple.

When the iPhone launched, a music player was integrated into a smartphone, and the need for a separate iPod rapidly weakened. Apple lost its iconic product of the time, but so what? The consumer was happy with even greater convenience; Apple was happy to lead the consumer into the new world.

And guess what? Microsoft also found its mojo again. Under a different leader, it abandoned the negativity and defensive posturing of its past and tried to refocus on its consumers—by playing long. It has become a cause again, not just a company. It is trying to deliver utility and benefits, not just numbers. And it shows. Great products are flowing again; new platforms are being built. It is neck and neck with Apple.

The iPhone, too, is no longer the best product out there. And yet it is the most desired. It, too, will fade away, replaced by something better, and those doing the fading will most likely be the folks at Apple—as long as they stay focused on the long game. If Apple also plays short-term, it will eventually run out of ideas.

What about you and your organization? What game are you in? Does your leader ever talk—sincerely—about cause and purpose, or just whip everyone into a fear-filled and greed-driven frenzy about targets and deliverables? Are your meetings fixated on benchmarking and catching up with your competitors, or on your own unique plays?

Does everything change when the CEO changes, or are CEOs selected to continue the distinctive values and timeless ethos of the organization? Is your strategy stuck in former glories and antiquated norms, or does it stay ahead of the curve by anticipating the needs of the future?

I often urge my clients to think about a twenty-five-year strategy, not a five-year one. Why twenty-five years? Twenty-five years is a whole generation. Few of us can expect to be around in the organization in twenty-five years. What would we strategize for if we knew we wouldn't be around to see the benefits? What investments would we make today that are more about the continuity of our work rather than its immediate payoffs?

There are few takers for the twenty-five-year strategy.

And that's very revealing. Most people are indeed caught in the finite game—the one of taking market share from competitors, of hitting stretch targets, of clocking big personal bonuses, of moving into the corner office and getting the nicer car.

A twenty-five-year strategy would be very different. It would aim to continue the play, not just to win the next few plays. It would play the long game, not just record some great quarters. It would aim to be around for generations by the simple expedients of staying *useful* and *relevant*.

Such a strategy would not be focused on itself. It would be focused on the benefits to others—the recipients and beneficiaries of the work and the products that flow from the strategy. The strategy would be bigger than itself, and so it would retire and refresh itself as necessary.

How Big Is Your Deal?

The Bigger Deal was the title of my last book, and it was all about things that are bigger than us, and that outlast us.

The best strategy is crafted in service of a bigger deal.

Are you working on anything whose benefits are far, far bigger than any rewards that accrue to you personally?

Are you working on anything whose impacts will outlast you?

Those are our only shots at meaning: to get out of our small selves and short lives, and to play bigger and longer.

The truly great strategies of human history are not those that offer a minor gain to a small group of people.

Mahatma Gandhi's strategy of nonviolent protest against the British occupation of India and accommodation of minority religions cost him his own life. But it gave self-determination to India's teeming multitudes and outlasted him.

Nelson Mandela's twenty-seven long and painful years in prison became the masterstroke that gave him the moral authority to unite and heal his nation.

Wangari Maathai's fight for her nation's trees was not about herself; it was about protecting the environment for the benefit of generations to come.

CEOs everywhere are very good at trumpeting "our people are our greatest asset" and "our business is centered on customers," but is there any real truth there? Why, then, are staff tossed out in every downturn, and customers gouged in the absence of meaningful competition?

Way too many companies are just vehicles for maximizing the returns to principal shareholders and senior executives, period. Customers are the suckers tricked into supplying the money; employees are the resources deployed to provide the labor. The real returns accrue upstairs.

A great business doesn't look anything like that. A great business follows the golden rule: it does things for the greater good of as many people as possible; and it aims to stick around for centuries, not just a few explosive years.

In fact, modern business leaders should learn a great deal from nature. A business is an ecosystem that aims to keep many elements in harmony. Imbalance in the shared value system causes the entire setup to collapse, eventually.

Human endeavor is not just about creating strategies that reward a few people with higher numbers. It is about enrolling citizens and employees in a collective purpose, in which they participate with enthusiasm and shared meaning. It is not just about selling to customers, but bonding with them in a shared belief system. It is about spreading rewards and leaving no one behind.

Sadly, that's not how most of the world works today. We only sing these noble things in churches and temples and at PR events, but we walk out ready to maximize personal gain in the shortest time possible, whatever it takes.

A great business follows the golden rule: it does things for the greater good of as many people as possible; and it aims to stick around for centuries, not just a few explosive years.

So if you wonder why we can't save our trees and elephants, or why we can't deal with global poverty and insecurity, wonder no longer. It's because we are not focused on the greater good for the greater time. It's why we have angry and frustrated masses everywhere, and why the elite are increasingly jittery and scared.

Our strategies should play for bigger deals than that.

Think about it. What would it take for your organization to be around in twenty-five years' time? What would it take to be around *and* going strong?

Only the bigger deals—with greater impact, and greater shared reward—bestow longevity.

Extreme Listening

A good strategist listens. Really listens.

Most of us, however, listen for signals that lead to personal gain. Or for confirmation of our already held beliefs. We hear what we want to hear.

Deeyah Khan makes documentary movies. In a recent one, *White Right*, she, a Muslim woman, spends time with white supremacists—not to expose or ridicule them, but to understand them. What she discovered was a group of people angry because they can't be heard—and once someone listened to them, their poisoned narrative began to unravel. She did an earlier film about fundamentalist jihadis and found the same insecurities and feelings of emasculation—manifesting as violence.

In a podcast interview with Simon Sinek in 2020, she pointed out that we all think we are the good guys! Even when people do terrible things, the story in their head does not tell them they're doing terrible things. They think they are doing the *right* thing, the *righteous* thing. Everyone thinks they are on the side of right.

We would do better to engage in empathetic listening. Not accusing people of being evil, but trying to understand *why* they do what they do.

This is extreme listening. Deeyah Khan spends time with some of the world's most maligned people, not to belittle them, but to understand them. Through the listening, she comes up with different ways to solve the problem of polarization and hatred, ways that revert to our shared humanity.

That there is strategy with a bigger deal in play.

Back to Dust

Customer: "I need a rope."
Shopkeeper: "What's it for?"
Customer: "Suicide."
Shopkeeper: "That will be five dollars."
Customer: "What? That's too much. I'll buy it elsewhere."
Shopkeeper: "What does it matter to you? You're about to die anyway!"

That was a scene from a movie I watched decades ago. I laughed at the time, but years later I reflected on the exchange. What does it tell us about ourselves?

Our interactions with most other people are just transactions. One side of the transaction must protect its gains and its profit margins; the other must recoil at any suspicion of being overcharged. The actual need behind the transaction is ignored, and irrelevant.

Why would the shopkeeper not react with sympathy, rather than see a chance to make a quick buck? Why would he not try to talk the customer out of his intention? And why would the customer not let the shopkeeper have his profit, since he would be departing anyway?

Because we have wired ourselves to maximize our gains from everything we do, big and small, that's why. We don't see the human being, only the net gain or loss. Even when a death is looming, we are maximizing.

The one place people do sometimes stop to take stock is the funeral. I heard a comedian say the other day: at funerals everyone becomes a philosopher. When staring at the dead body of someone known to them, they say things like, "You can't take it with you," or "In the end, the only property we own is that six-foot casket."

The mourners gain some profundity; they see something bigger than their material belongings.

But immediately upon departing the funeral, the very same people can be found loudly haggling about the taxi fare, or making phone calls on their mobiles to make sure they got the right price on some deal or other. The philosophy only lasts as long as the funeral does.

It would serve us well to reflect on our own insignificance throughout our lives. Not just when confronted with the deaths of others, or our own mortality, but always.

Consider my translation of these classic lines from Bābā Farīd, renowned Sufi poet and mystic, as he gazes upon a burial:

Look Farīd.
The dust has been opened
And dust is being spilled on dust.
The dust that used to laugh
The dust that used to cry
Is now back to dust.
Just dust.
Look Farīd.

Even in our happiest moments, we are but dust. It is dust that laughs. Even in our times of triumph, we are merely dust. Even when we score the winning deal through the epic strategy, it is only dust that wins, and it wins only dust. And when we lie defeated, we get a premonition of where we will eventually lie. Back in the dust.

This recognition would help us make better sense of our lives. It would help us stay grounded, stay humble, and place our wins and losses in perspective. The recognition that we are nothing would, paradoxically, help us to actually become something.

We are merely passing through this life; we are merely taking a shape. If we must maximize something, let those things be compassion and goodwill—the things that make us better than just dust.

Kick up some dust now, and look at it. Recognize yourself.

Then go make strategies that matter.

THANK YOU

A book like this one does not emerge only from the author's own head; it is the result of multitudes of interactions with thinkers, leaders, and practitioners over many years.

I appreciate the many client organizations and their leaders who have given me a unique vantage point from which to study strategy—by being right there where it happens. Those experiences were invaluable over the years and helped me see patterns and connections that I otherwise would not have.

We also become better by having role models. I have served under two leaders who brought clarity to my own thinking: Rosemary Radcliffe, who would understand complex situations effortlessly and lay down a way to address them almost instinctively; and Naval Sood, who showed me the value of rigor and attention to detail, even when using imagination and creativity.

My thanks as always to my editors at the Nation Media Group, who have always given me the space to write freely and exuberantly on their pages. Many of the thoughts about strategy contained in this book emerged first as strands in my weekly columns.

Last, heartfelt thanks to the project managers, editors, and designers at Girl Friday Productions, who turned a manuscript into the book now in your hands.

AUTHOR'S NOTE

Strategy is a way of dealing with uncertainty and complexity. I have highlighted the successful and not-so-successful strategies of many organizations in this book. At different times in their histories, firms can be seen to enjoy periods of great success (when their strategies pay off, sometimes through foresight, often through serendipity). That should not be taken to mean they will *always* be successful. A successful strategy works in a given situation at a given time, not in perpetuity. Those situations do change; missteps will happen. Getting strategy right in a given period is no guarantee of future success, so nothing in this book should be taken as a blanket endorsement of any particular company or product. Indeed, unless organizations stay grounded and humble and are willing to refresh their thinking, past successes can themselves herald a fall by breeding hubris and complacency.

YOU'VE READ THE BOOK, NOW DO THE COURSE!

If you enjoyed *Up & Ahead* and gained a fresh and simple way of thinking strategically, you may want to take it a step further.

Sunwords gives you an easy way of learning and applying the Strategy Four-Stepper with a peer group of enthusiastic participants.

Our virtual course, Think Like a Strategist, gathers diverse and interesting people to go deeper with strategy. You will learn how to apply the lessons in a practical team project to devise a strategy from scratch.

Think Like a Strategist is taught and led by Sunny personally. It is highly interactive, fun, and lively. Join our Zoom class from anywhere in the world!

For more details and to register now, visit:

https://sunwords.com/the-4by4-leader/think-like-a -strategist/

Ping us at hello@sunwords.com to find out more.

THE GIANTS AND THEIR SHOULDERS

These are the folks who have inspired my understanding of strategy. I owe them an enormous debt of gratitude for shaping and provoking my own thinking.

Richard Rumelt
Roger Martin
Michael Porter
Rita McGrath
Henry Mintzberg
John Kay
Margaret Heffernan
Tom Peters
Bill Taylor
Scott Galloway
Youngme Moon
Seth Godin

FURTHER READING

If you want to go deeper with strategy, here are some of the books I have found to be worth reading:

- » *Strategy Bites Back* by Henry Mintzberg, Bruce W. Ahlstrand, and Joseph Lampel (Pearson PTR, 2005)
- » *Radical Uncertainty* by John Kay and Mervyn King (W. W. Norton and Company, 2020)
- » *Uncharted* by Margaret Heffernan (Simon & Schuster, 2020)
- » *Good Strategy/Bad Strategy* by Richard Rumelt (Currency, 2011)
- » *Seeing Around Corners* by Rita McGrath (Mariner Books, 2019)
- » *Superforecasting* by Philip Tetlock and Dan Gardner (Crown, 2015)
- » *Different* by Youngme Moon (Crown Business, 2010)
- » *Playing to Win* by A. G. Lafley and Roger Martin (HBR Press, 2013)

- » *Excellence Now: Extreme Humanism* by Tom Peters (Networlding Publishing, 2021)
- » *The Infinite Game* by Simon Sinek (Portfolio, 2019)

THE AUTHOR

Sunny Bindra works as a "sense maker"—he helps leaders and organizations understand their worlds and succeed in them.

He is a business advisor, writer, educator, and public speaker, delivering his own brand of advisory services and unique business content. He advises chief executives and chairpersons in a select group of leading companies, helping them to develop strategic thinking and make radical change happen.

His clients have ranged from giant banking groups to unusual start-ups; from those running transport networks in London to those managing disasters in

Hawaii. He has advised on mergers and acquisitions in the UK and on strategy across Africa.

Sunny is the founder of Fast Forward, a leadership development program with a strong following among the region's elite business leaders, and The 4BY4 Leader, a new set of online courses for young professionals.

This is his fourth book.

www.sunwords.com
@sunnysunwords
Sunwords by Sunny Bindra